LIFE IS _____.

GOD'S ILLOGICAL LOVE WILL CHANGE YOUR EXISTENCE

Study Guide

JUDAH SMITH

WITH JUSTIN JAQUITH

NELSON
BOOKS

An Imprint of Thomas Nelson

Published in Nashville, Tennessee, by Nelson Books, an imprint of Thomas Nelson. Nelson Books and Thomas Nelson are registered trademarks of HarperCollins Christian Publishing, Inc.

ISBN 978-0-718-03071-1

First Printing December 2014 / Printed in the United States of America

CONTENTS

How to Use This Guide

Life Is _____.

How would you fill in that blank?

Several years ago, our church launched a campaign to get our city of Seattle to think about Jesus. We put a similar phrase, "Jesus Is _____", on billboards, bus signs, and bumper magnets. We invited people to fill in the blank for themselves on our website, jesus-is.org.

Thousands of responses came in. The answers reflected what the people of Seattle thought about God and where they were on their spiritual journeys.

Thinking about who Jesus is led me to the premise of this book: we can live life to the fullest only through Jesus.

We all ask questions about the meaning of our lives, what we are here for, and what is truly important. We all have our own answers to those questions. For me, it all comes back to Jesus. He is the perfect example of a life well lived, and he is the source of authentic, refreshing, satisfying life for us.

The goal of this small-group study is to help you find fulfillment in life by looking at what God says about it in the Bible. Small groups are a great place to go through the material in the *Life Is* _____ book, this study guide, and the videos. To this end, the following will provide you with a few ideas on how to most effectively organize and facilitate your group time.

Group Size

The *Life Is* _____ video curriculum is designed to be experienced in a group setting such as a Bible study, Sunday school class, or any small group gathering. After viewing the video together, members will participate in a group discussion. Ideally, this group should be between five and fifteen people. If your group is much larger, consider breaking into two or more groups.

Materials Needed

Each participant should have his or her own study guide, which includes video teaching questions, small group discussion questions, and daily personal studies to deepen learning between sessions.

Facilitation

Each group should have a facilitator who is responsible for starting the video and for keeping track of time during discussions and activities. Facilitators may also read questions aloud and monitor discussions, inviting the group to respond and ensuring that everyone has a chance to participate.

Between-Sessions Personal Study

During the week, you can maximize the impact of the course with the daily personal studies provided. For each video session, there are five short studies with accompanying questions that will help you think about and apply that week's topic to your life.

Each study can be completed in about twenty minutes. The studies are personal and devotional in nature, so feel free to utilize them in whatever way works best for you and your schedule. You may wish to read one each day or complete the entire week in one sitting.

If you are unable to finish your between-sessions study, still attend the group study video session! We are all busy and life happens. You are still wanted and welcome at class, even if you don't have your "homework" done.

LIFE IS <u>to be loved by God</u>

Welcome

Welcome to the first session of *Life Is* ____. For the next six weeks, you will be exploring with your group how to find true fulfillment and significance in life.

During this first week, you will discover with your group how "life is ... to be loved by God." Being aware of God's love is *foundational* for everything we do in life. It is a truth that will change your perspective about yourself, about others, and about life itself.

Whether you have been following Jesus for years or aren't even sure God exists, you are welcome on this journey. The group will provide a safe place for you to think, share, and ask questions as you work through the topics. It will provide a place where you can belong, no matter what stage of the journey you are on. It's going to be an amazing few weeks.

As we begin today, find someone near you — a friend or maybe someone you've never met before — and ask each other the following questions:

- Have you ever been lost before? Describe the event briefly.
- How did you feel when you realized you were lost?
- How did you feel when you finally found your way?

Video Teaching

The following are a few key thoughts to note as you watch session one of the video. Use the space provided to jot down personal observations or applications.

Love is the major theme of this life and our existence. And not just any love, but God's love for you and for me. Our significance and our identity can be summed up in the word *love*.

Life starts not with our love but with us being loved — with us discovering how much God loves us.

In John 3:16 we read, "God so loved the world" (NIV). That includes *bad* people. In fact, God is obsessed with evil, sinful, bad people. His love for us is passionate and even illogical. He loves us whether we recognize and reciprocate his love or not.

Love finds its maximum expression in Jesus. Jesus died for us at the chance — at the mere *possibility* — that we would accept him. God gave Jesus to us with no strings attached and with no guarantees. This is how risky and ridiculous God's love for humanity is.

Life begins with us realizing the value we have before God. He is obsessed with us. He knows every detail and every nook and cranny of our lives.

The story of Hosea and Gomer in the Old Testament is one of the most beautiful and scandalous pictures of what God has done for humanity. It illustrates his shocking, relentless love for you and for me. We already belong to God, yet he paid to buy back what was already his — and the price he paid was the life of his son, Jesus.

We find our value not in things, status, and influence, but in the fact that the most powerful being in the universe is completely obsessed with us. He desires for *all* people to come to know him.

We have the privilege to tell people everywhere about the unconditional, relentless love of God for them.

Our journey during these next few weeks begins not with us trying to figure out things using our own intellect, but with Jesus and with God's love. It begins with the one who cares about us at our best and at our worst.

Group Discussion

Take a few moments to discuss the following questions with your group.

1. Have you ever wondered what life is all about? What answers did you come up with? What answers have you heard from others?

2. How important is love to human beings? Why do you think it is so important?

3. Why is God's love for us more important than any other kind of love — including our love for him?

4. What does the phrase "God so loved the world" in John 3:16 tell us about God's love? How big is his love? Who does he love?

5. How is God's love different from the love we usually receive and give to each other here on earth?

6. How does the fact that Jesus became a man show us that God is interested in our existence and in the details of our lives?

7. In the story of Hosea and Gomer, who does Hosea represent? Who does Gomer represent? What does this story tell us about God's love toward us?

8. When it comes to sharing Jesus with other people, what is the essence of our message? What do we tell them about his love?

Closing Prayer

Close your time together in prayer. Here are a few ideas of what you could pray about based on the topic of this session:

- Pray that God will guide you on your journey of discovery with Jesus, regardless of where you are in the process.
- Pray that you will really understand and believe how much God loves you.
- Pray that God's love would be real to you in your daily activities — that you would think about it, enjoy it, and let it affect your emotions, words, and choices.
- Pray that you will be able to show God's love to other people this week.

Weekly Challenge

Sometime during the week — maybe even tomorrow morning — take this simple, practical step to help you put into words what God's love means for you:

Find a quiet place and spend a few minutes thinking about God's love. Write down your thoughts. It doesn't have to be polished, professional, or perfect — this is for your eyes only. For example, you could ask yourself:

- *What are some words that describe God's love?*
- *What is hard for me to understand or believe about his love?*
- *Have I seen his love in action in my life? In what ways?*

Then, if you're comfortable doing so, meet with another Jesus-follower, maybe even a member of this small group — over coffee, lunch, or even the phone — and share together your understanding of God's love and how that affects your life.

Recommended Reading

Review the introduction and chapters 1 and 2 in the book *Life Is* ____. Use the space provided to write any key points or questions you want to bring to the next group meeting.

Between-Sessions Personal Study

Day 1: Love and Corn Nuts

I overuse the word *love*. I have been informed of this on more than one occasion, and it's true. Love is a great concept and a great word, so I use it for everything and everyone. I love my wife. I love my kids. I love my friends. I love golf. I love carbs. I love the way I dress.

I love *love*.

Recently, I was carrying on a conversation with a friend when he interrupted me to point out that I had just used the word *love* in reference to my children and to Corn Nuts in the same sentence. Here's the problem: when I overuse the term *love*, I end up watering down its significance. My kids might start to feel like they are on the same level as Corn Nuts, for example.

The question becomes, if I love *everybody*, do I really love *anybody*? That is, don't I have to be selective with my love in order for it to be significant? Don't I have to reserve my love for certain people in my life?

It's kind of a trick question. As humans, we do tend to love selectively. We love people who are important to us, who are close to us, who love us back. We don't have the capacity to love everyone on the same level.

But God does. In John 3:16–17 we read:

For God so loved the world that He gave His only begotten Son, that whoever believes in Him should not perish but have everlasting life. For God did not send His Son into the world to condemn the world, but that the world through Him might be saved (NKJV).

God loves the *whole world*. Not just the good part of the world or the part of the world that would someday love him back, but the whole world.

God loves everyone, all the time, with a love so extravagant and generous that our human minds can't wrap around it. God's love is indiscriminate. It's illogical. It's never-ending. God loved us before we knew about him or cared about him, and he'll continue to love us whether we reciprocate that love or not.

When God says, "I love you," it's more than just a nice way to get you to close your eyes and go to sleep. It's not an empty phrase spoken out of habit or a spiritual obligation because he's God and he has to love everybody. It's a heartfelt expression of his passion for you.

We get to spend the rest of our lifetimes enjoying and exploring that love.

- Do you ever find yourself wondering if God really loves you? What concerns or doubts do you have about God's love for you?

- How is God's love better than typical human love?

- How does understanding God's love for you affect your day-to-day life?

Day 2: It's Not What You Do

One of the first questions people ask each other when they meet for the first time is, "What do you do?" What they are asking for, of course, is an occupation or job title.

I'm never sure how to answer this question. I'm a pastor first and foremost, but not everyone is comfortable with that title. When I introduce myself, some people look confused. Others look guilty, as if I see their secret sins and am judging them. Sometimes the atmosphere turns Arctic, and I can tell the person has had an unpleasant experience with church or with pastors in the past. Some people become hyper-religious. As soon as they hear I'm a pastor, they offer to pray for our dinner, and they pray with so much zeal, passion, and holy jargon that the roast chicken almost resurrects.

Actually, I disagree with the premise behind the question. Why is what we do so important? Why do we care so much about a person's occupation? Is that really what gives us value or makes us worth relating to?

Yes, I'm a pastor. But I'm also a speaker and a writer. I'm a husband and a father. I'm a golfer with delusions of grandeur and anger management issues. I'm a friend. I'm a Christian. I'm a work in progress. And that barely scratches the surface of who I really am.

My real problem with the whole "what do you do?" approach to relationship is that it's the exact opposite of God's approach. God's love doesn't start with what we do but with who he is. Here's how Paul describes it in a letter to the Christians at Rome:

> What shall we say about such wonderful things as these? If God is for us, who can ever be against us? Since he did not spare even his own Son but gave him up for us all, won't he

also give us everything else? Who dares accuse us whom God has chosen for his own? No one — for God himself has given us right standing with himself. Who then will condemn us? No one — for Christ Jesus died for us and was raised to life for us, and he is sitting in the place of honor at God's right hand, pleading for us ... I am convinced that nothing can ever separate us from God's love (Romans 8:31–34, 38).

God is love. Love isn't just what he does; it's who he is. And his love is directed toward you and me regardless of our behavior, our mood, or our response.

God loved us before we did anything. His love is not a function of what we do; it's an inevitable and unstoppable result of his nature.

What does that mean for us? It means we don't have to earn God's love. Some of us think that every time we pray we have to show God our résumé. We have to recite a list of our successes in order to convince God to be on our side. But we don't have to prove our worth to him.

Trust me, you can't impress God with what you do. Whatever you can do, Jesus can do it a whole lot better.

He already did it better, actually. Jesus lived the life we could never live: free from errors, faults, mistakes, and sins. He impressed God so we wouldn't have to. He lived free from sin because we would never have been able to.

When we put our trust in Jesus, his victory becomes ours. When he died on the cross, he took the penalty for our sins. We don't need to carry that weight anymore, because it went to the grave with Jesus.

Now we relate to God as if we had never sinned. Our mistakes are forgiven, forgotten, and forever gone. We are as righteous as

Jesus is in God's eyes. We don't need to impress God with what we do, because he's already more in love with us and more proud of us than we could ever comprehend.

God wants us to do our best and to live right. He's happy that we try to be good, and he's proud of our progress and our victories. But for better or for worse, our behavior doesn't alter his love. He loves us as much now as he'll ever love us.

So stop *doing* for a minute and just let God love you. It will change everything.

- Do you ever find yourself trying to talk God into helping you based on your efforts or merits? Why do you think you tend to take that approach?

- Paul writes in Romans 8:38 that "nothing can ever separate us from God's love." Do you ever have trouble believing God could love you? What situations in life could make you doubt God's love?

- How does relaxing and letting God love you unconditionally help you be a better person?

Day 3: Love Is a Person

According to every sci-fi movie I've ever seen (which isn't saying much), robots aren't supposed to have feelings. Fear, hate, happiness — and most of all, love — are human emotions.

Of course, because emotionless robots are boring, most of these movies also include an exception to the no-feelings rule. Take *WALL-E*, for example. I realize *WALL-E* probably doesn't qualify as a sci-fi movie for most people, but when you have three young kids, that's about as edgy as it gets.

In the movie, the main character is a robot who can't speak, but he still conveys his love for a fellow robot in a way that makes you think he's almost human. Despite being basically a tin can with circuit boards and lights, you identify with him, cheer for him, and even love him back. Why? Because he loves, and his love draws you in.

Now, for all you pet lovers out there, I realize emo-robots aren't the only creatures with feelings. Animals can love too. Or so I'm told. I do not speak from personal experience, because I have issues with pets. More specifically, I have issues with slobber and hair and bodily functions and howling and things that crawl in bed with me at night uninvited.

But animals and robots aside, I am convinced that love is first and foremost a human emotion. We love because we are humans, and because we are humans, we love.

It's no accident that we are wired this way. Love is part of who we are because we were created in God's image. God is love, and love is a reflection of God:

> Dear friends, let us continue to love one another, for love comes from God. Anyone who loves is a child of God and knows God. But anyone who does not love does not know God, for God is love (1 John 4:7–8).

God's love is far more than a concept or a philosophy or a chemical reaction. That's where a lot of us get hung up. We try to visualize God's love, but his love is so much bigger than ours that we can't figure out how to apply it to our lives.

So here's the bottom line. God's love is a person, and his name is Jesus.

When Jesus came to this planet, he didn't just talk about love, preach about love, and demonstrate love. He *was* love. He was God's love in physical, tangible form. He didn't have to *try* to love bad people — it was the most natural thing in the world for him, because he was and is love.

Many of us can probably talk about God's love on a doctrinal level, but can we imagine Jesus walking up to us and giving us a big hug? That thought actually makes some people feel uncomfortable. Why? Maybe it seems undignified, or maybe they don't feel worthy.

But that's exactly the point. Jesus shows us just how real and tangible and practical God's love is. His love is aimed directly at you and me even when — especially when — we are at our lowest point.

If you're having trouble believing that God loves you, or if you can't quite visualize what God's love looks like, just look at Jesus. Think about Jesus. Get to know Jesus in your day-to-day existence.

When you meet Jesus, you meet love.

- Is it hard for you to visualize God's love? Why?

- What does the phrase "God is love" mean to you?

- How does knowing Jesus help you understand God's love?

- How does knowing Jesus help you show love to other people?

Day 4: When Love Hides

My wife, Chelsea, and I have been married for fifteen years, and our marriage and our love are stronger than ever. I deserve approximately five percent of the credit for this. Anyone who knows us will tell you that Chelsea is the reason our marriage is so amazing. I'm a lucky man.

You learn a lot about love when you've been married for fifteen years. For one thing, you learn that love is way more than just being with someone who makes you happy. Stand-up comedians make me happy, but I don't love them. Massage techs at those airport massage stands make me happy, but I don't love them. Happy feelings are great, and marriage should generally be a happy experience, but happiness by itself is superficial and even selfish compared to true love.

You also learn a lot about conflict resolution when you've been married for fifteen years. That's another term for *fighting*, but it sounds better. Specifically, you learn what *not* to say in the heat of the battle. Which is pretty much anything except, "I'm sorry, it was my fault." Just kidding. Actually, I'm not.

There are good ways and bad ways to deal with conflicts in any relationship. Learning to "fight right" will literally save your marriage and your friendships. Sometimes people think conflict is a sign that love has died. I think conflict proves love is stronger than ever. Here's why. If we didn't love the person with whom we are disagreeing, we would just walk away. *Ain't nobody got time for that.*

But we do love that person, so we stick around and work through the messiness that is love. That's when true love shines. Our love is strongest when our feelings are weakest.

One of the keys to marital success is to be able to trust love even when we can't see it or feel it or understand it. The same goes for our walk with God. I wish I could say that our relationship with God will always be happy. But just like any other relationship, there will be tense, confusing, and seemingly contradictory moments.

In those times, it can be tempting to conclude that God doesn't love us. We don't feel his love. We don't see his love. Things are happening that don't seem congruent with a God who is love.

God knows that life can feel this way. This is why the apostle John — who is called the "apostle of love" because he is so famous for his understanding of God's love — wrote this:

All who declare that Jesus is the Son of God have God living in them, and they live in God. We know how much God loves us, and we have put our trust in his love (1 John 4:15–16).

Trust God's love, even when you can't see it. Trust his love for *you*. Trust that he is on your side, that he is with you, that he is for you, that he cares about your pain, and that he is actively working to meet your needs. Don't ever give up on his love.

Here's the crazy part. Even if you *do* give up on his love, he never gives up on you. He loved you before you loved him, and he'll love you to the end of your days whether you respond to him or not.

Sometimes life is a mystery. Bad things happen to everyone. But that doesn't change the fact that God's love is directed at you right now in your pain, in your hurt, in your mistakes, in your weaknesses. Maybe at this moment you don't feel loved. But someday you will look back and see God's love in this moment and every moment of your story.

Remember, there's more to your life than what you see around you. Someday, God will wipe away all tears. He will deal with hurt and pain and loneliness and grief and death once and for all. And one thing will remain: his unfailing love.

None of us can explain everything about this life, but we can trust in God's love.

- How is love different from happiness?

- Describe a time in your life when you didn't feel God's love. How did you get through that time? Did that experience ultimately help or hurt your relationship with God?

- After reading 1 John 4:15–16, what does it mean to you to "put [your] trust in God's love"?

- Does your understanding of heaven help you walk through difficult times in this life? In what way?

Day 5: Dirty Laundry

I don't do laundry. It's not my fault. I've tried — believe me, I have. But when I open the hamper and see a mound of soiled apparel that has been marinating for days, I am physically incapable of touching it. It's a convenient OCD issue, and I'm in no hurry to be cured.

I also can't stand to wear anything dirty. So I am forever dependent on others to wash my clothes. Luckily for me, Chelsea and I married young, so I never had to experience the laundry limbo that is bachelorhood. My mom did my laundry before; my wife does it now.

I sense some of you judging me. It's not selfish or sexist. It's survival.

Anyway, I remember once as a teenager looking for clothes and being frustrated because I had nothing to wear. Actually, in the interest of full disclosure, I had a closet full of clothes, but the outfits I wanted to wear happened to be dirty.

At the time, besides my mom and sister, my aunt was staying

with us. I came down the stairs and yelled, "With all the women in this house, what does it take to get some clean clothes?"

Not one of my brightest moments.

There was a tangible silence. I thought about what I had just said. In hindsight, I probably should have thought about it before saying it. But, like I said, it was not one of my better moments.

I should mention: you don't mess with my mom. She's an incredible person with a boundless capacity to love, but she has absolutely no problem informing people — especially her offspring — when they need to change in some area.

My comment did not go over well with her, for obvious reasons. I don't remember the specific punishment I received. I've effectively blocked it from my mind. It might come out with therapy. But I do remember the fear, the terror, and the dread that I felt when I realized she was coming for me. Clearly, I had made a mistake.

There is something about making a mistake that instantly instills fear in our hearts. Perhaps it's because we experienced consequences from parents and other authorities in our lives when we've made mistakes. Or perhaps it's because we know how upset we get when others fail us.

The consequences of our mistakes motivate us to improve, so in that sense, the fear or embarrassment that we feel can actually produce good things. But we were not created to have a lifestyle of fear and shame — especially when it comes to our relationship with God. Jesus came to earth to demonstrate a different kind of relationship: one based on love, not on fear.

For the last couple of days, we've been reading from John's description of God's amazing love. John continues:

God is love, and all who live in love live in God, and God lives in them. And as we live in God, our love grows more perfect. So we will not be afraid on the day of judgment, but we can face him with confidence because we live like Jesus here in this world. Such love has no fear, because perfect love expels all fear. If we are afraid, it is for fear of punishment, and this shows that we have not fully experienced his perfect love (1 John 4:16–18).

Sure, we might say. *It's easy for Jesus to live without fear. He was perfect. But I'm a mess. There's no way God could love me like this.*

The good news is that it's not our performance or our holiness that earns God's love. He loves us because he created us and because it's his nature to love. Through Jesus, we are free to be loved by him and to love him back.

That's the point of the cross. We died to ourselves and became alive in Jesus. Our lives are hidden in him. That means that as he is, so are we. He is perfect in God's eyes: so are we. He is loved by God: so are we. He can come boldly before God's presence: so can we.

When we come to know God's love, our fear of punishment disappears. Ironically, we also find ourselves more motivated than ever to live a life that pleases him. The love of God in Jesus is a far greater motivation than fear is when it comes to living right.

Yes, we make mistakes. We mess up. We sin. But God is not storing up his anger against us. He's not waiting for an opportune moment to drop the hammer. His thoughts toward us are thoughts of love, acceptance, mercy, and reconciliation.

We can enjoy God without fear because we are truly, deeply, fully loved.

- In your experience, is love or fear a stronger force? Why?

- Do you tend to think more about God's love or your mistakes? Why do you think that is the case?

- John writes, "As we live in God, our love grows more perfect" (1 John 4:17). How has your understanding of God's love changed since you first heard about or met God for yourself?

- If you live in God's love rather than living in fear of punishment, will you sin more or less? Why?

LIFE IS to love others

Welcome

Welcome to session two of *Life Is* ____. This week, you will explore with your group how "life is ... to love others." Once you understand God's amazing love for you, your natural desire will be to reflect that love to others.

Most of us would like to be more loving. We'd like to be people who genuinely, generously love God and others. But often that's easier said than done.

The problem with becoming loving people is that we often think we have to change ourselves. We think it's up to us to love more and to love better. In the process, we find ourselves becoming frustrated because, even though we might not like to admit it, we all tend to be a bit selfish at the core.

That's where Jesus comes in. The only true answer to loving others is to focus on Jesus first.

As you get started today, take a few moments to meet a few people in the room whom you haven't met before or simply don't know well. Find out their names, their favorite hobbies, and what they are enjoying most about the group.

As an option, you can also play the following game. One person begins by standing in the center of the group. That person chooses someone from the group and then declares his or her love in the most exaggerated way possible. At the same time, the chosen person attempts to keep a straight face. If the chosen person smiles or laughs, he or she takes the place of the person in the center of the group, and the game continues. Play a few rounds and then move into the video teaching.

Video Teaching

The following are a few key thoughts to note as you watch session two of the video. Use the space provided to jot down personal observations or applications.

The secret to loving others is learning to love Jesus.

In Mark 8:34, Jesus said, "Whoever wants to be my disciple must deny themselves and take up their cross and follow me" (NIV). This was a radical, extreme image. Crosses represented pain, torture, and death.

It is imperative that we understand the true pathway to life according to Jesus. He teaches that if we want to find life and satisfaction and fulfillment, we have to lose our lives. We have to completely commit to self-denial, yielding, and surrendering.

We naturally think about ourselves all the time. We are subconsciously consumed with self. Yet Jesus teaches that a life focused on self will never be fulfilling.

This is not about us denying ourselves. It's not even about us following Jesus. It's not about us at all — it's about Jesus.

We forget about self as we become enamored with Jesus. Our tendency is to focus on what we have to do and on what our part is — when in reality our part is just to respond to Jesus' love for us.

The gospel is about God's love, not about our love or sacrifice. We simply get caught up in the fact he gave his life for us.

When we focus on Jesus, our lives naturally reflect his love and generosity. We become selfless, noble, giving people — without us hardly trying or noticing.

Abundant life has nothing to do with nice clothes, fine cars, or other external things, but with peace and wholeness on the inside.

We make a daily decision to shift our focus to Jesus.

In the book of Acts, we read how the early church, because of its focus on Jesus, was known everywhere as a community of great generosity and love.

Stephen was an average, ordinary person who was so in love with Jesus that he was able to forgive and love even the people who were murdering him. That sounds a lot like Jesus. When we focus on Jesus, we learn to love humanity as Jesus does.

Group Discussion

Take a few moments to discuss the following questions with your group.

1. Have you ever felt frustrated with your lack of ability to love God or to love other people? If so, what did you try to do differently to change that?

2. Why do you think Jesus used the imagery of the cross when he talked about following him?

3. What does self-denial mean to you? How does Jesus' message of following him differ from what people often think of when they talk about self-denial and self-discipline?

4. Why is it important to make following Jesus more about Jesus than about us?

5. When we follow Jesus and focus on him, what naturally happens to our lifestyle and our character?

6. What is most inspiring to you about the early church in the book of Acts?

7. What does Stephen's attitude toward his murderers tell you about his walk with Jesus? How did his relationship with Jesus influence his life?

Closing Prayer

Close your time together in prayer. Here are a few ideas of what you could pray about based on the topic of this session:

- Pray that in a real and practical way you will be aware of Jesus' love for you throughout your day.
- Pray that your life will be less about self and more about Jesus.
- Pray that people who come in contact with you will see Jesus through you.
- Pray that you will have wisdom and grace to let God's love shine through you to difficult people in your world.
- Pray that God's love will become a defining characteristic of your life.

Weekly Challenge

Sometime this week, sit down and make a list — mental or written — of the people you are around regularly. Chances are, you really do love some of them. And chances are, you don't get along well with some of them. That's life.

Now, look at your list. Instead of resolving to force yourself to get along with the difficult people in your world, take a moment to reflect on God's love toward you. Ask yourself, *How much does God love me when I'm a difficult person? How much does he love me when I do selfish things? How badly do I need God's unconditional love?*

Before you return to your normal routine, take a moment to think about how much God loves the people in your life. What does he think about them? Does his love change based on their performance?

For the rest of the week, when you happen to run into these people — especially the difficult ones — try to keep God's love for them at the forefront of your mind. You probably won't bat a thousand, and that's okay. But if you focus on Jesus, and if you make your encounters with people less about self and more about naturally reflecting God's love, you'll be amazed how much easier it is to live a life of love.

Recommended Reading

Review chapters 3 and 4 in the book *Life Is* _____. Use the space provided to write any key points or questions you want to bring to the next group meeting.

Between-Sessions Personal Study

Day 1: Loved People Love People

Recently I bought a new swimsuit. In my defense, I only bought it because Chelsea loved it. That's my disclaimer. This particular swimsuit was not a style I had ever owned before, but I had been seeing it around lately. You couldn't call it a Speedo, per se, because the cut was more like traditional swim trunks. But it was definitely tight. Some might even say form-fitting.

We were on vacation as a family the first time I actually wore my new suit in public. Our kids were already down at the pool when I walked up. Instantly, my oldest child came running across the patio. "Dad!" he hissed. "What are you wearing?"

My second-born was even more direct. And loud. "You're wearing underwear!"

Ouch. You have to understand that up until this point, to my kids, I was the fashion hero. I was the style expert, the person they went to for advice.

But not this time. They clearly felt I needed a wardrobe intervention.

Their comments stung, so I found myself fighting back. Very maturely. "Oh, yeah? Well, you — you — don't even have chest hair yet. So zip it, kids."

Needless to say, the shorts have not made a second public appearance.

So, what do tight swimsuits have to do with the love of Jesus? It's probably a bit of a stretch (sorry … couldn't resist), but here's what I noticed in this situation. My kids made fun of me, so my instant, unthinking, defensive reaction was to make fun of them. It was lighthearted, but it illustrates how we as humans often deal with negativity: by propagating it.

You've probably heard the phrase, "Hurt people hurt people." It means that if you find someone who is continually hurting others, chances are he or she has been deeply hurt in the past. The negative actions are a reflection of the pain, loneliness, and hopelessness the person feels inside.

That might be a human tendency, but it doesn't describe Jesus. He didn't think like that or react like that. Not even once.

If anyone had the right to push back, fight back, and lash out, it was Jesus. Jesus was perfect. Literally. He did nothing but good during his time on earth. But he was jailed on trumped-up charges, publicly humiliated, slandered and lied about, and, ultimately, executed.

The hurt he experienced, however, became his greatest act of love. He refused to propagate hate. He stopped the cycle of pain with the power of love.

That changes everything. Because Jesus loves me, I can love others. Because he accepts me, I can accept others. When I look at people from a perspective of love and understanding, it helps me show them mercy. It motivates me to be an agent of healing instead of revenge.

In the New Testament, Peter talks about this exact principle:

For God called you to do good, even if it means suffering, just as Christ suffered for you. He is your example, and you must follow in his steps. He never sinned, nor ever deceived anyone. He did not retaliate when he was insulted, nor threaten revenge when he suffered. He left his case in the hands of God, who always judges fairly. He personally carried our sins in his body on the cross so that we can be dead to sin and live for what is right. By his wounds you are healed (1 Peter 2:21–24).

I am not saying that people aren't responsible for their actions. We all choose how to respond to whatever life throws our way. Just because we've been hurt doesn't mean we are obligated to hurt others. But looking at people through love has an amazing way of softening our responses.

It's true that hurt people often hurt people. But that's not the end of the story. Because Jesus loves us, we can propagate love. Our hurt can become a vehicle to understand people, love people, and have compassion for people. We can be hurt people who help people.

We've all been hurt, but that just means we can all be bigger, better people. Here's what I've found: loved people love people. Restored people restore people. Accepted people accept people. Valued people value people. So let's choose to live in God's love, and hurt will never hold us back again.

Now I'm going to go shopping for a new swimsuit.

- Have you ever been deeply hurt by someone? Did that affect the way you treated future relationships? How?

- Has God ever loved you when you didn't deserve it? How does that make you feel?

- Peter wrote, "By his wounds you are healed" (1 Peter 2:24). What does that mean to you? How can you use Jesus' love to bring healing to others?

- How did Jesus react when people hurt him? How does thinking about Jesus' love change the way you react to mean people?

Day 2: Bacon, Squirrels, Love

Do you ever get fixated on a particular thing to the point that you can't think about anything else? Maybe it's a hobby, or a project at school, or a situation at work. Suddenly, everything in life seems to revolve around that one thing.

That is how my brain works most of the time, actually. For better or for worse, I am by nature obsessive-compulsive. Either I like something or I hate it, and if you happen to cross my path, I'm going to try to talk you into believing the way I do at that particular moment. But a few days or weeks or months down the road, I will lose interest in whatever I was obsessed with and move on to the next thing.

It drives Chelsea bats.

For example, I used to hate bacon. I know, that sounds almost unpatriotic. "Pigs don't sweat," someone once told me, "so all those toxins get stored up in the meat you are eating." That was enough to turn me off of bacon forever.

Or so I thought. Then an NFL player I know started telling me about the difference between good fats and bad fats. Long story short, I now eat bacon. Lots of it. I am convinced bacon is proof that God loves us and wants us to be happy.

But I won't eat bananas, because that same football player convinced me they are of the Devil. Something about messing with your insulin levels.

The lesson in all this is that what we focus on has a way of running our lives. Mine is run by bacon, and I'm okay with that.

This is why I do not ride motorcycles. I've heard that when you are riding a motorcycle, you always steer toward whatever you are looking at. I'm sure I'd be riding along, and I'd be like, "Look, a squirrel!" That wouldn't end well for me, the bike, or the squirrel. So I stay with vehicles with four wheels, and even then I try to get someone else to drive.

When it comes to relationships, I think all of us want to be kind, loving, unselfish people. We know God loves us, and we want to love others as well. We have great intentions.

But we focus on the wrong thing. We tell ourselves, *Don't be selfish. Don't think about what you want. Sacrifice. Work harder. Love more. Come on, just be a better person already!* Like the motorcycle example, we steer our lives right at the thing we are trying to avoid. We end up doing the opposite of what we wanted to do.

The problem is that "self" — to state the obvious — is inherently selfish. So, if we try to fix *ourselves* and change *ourselves* by *ourselves*, we'll only end up more fixated on *self* than ever. It's a plan doomed to fail.

In Romans 7, Paul describes the frustration of wanting to do one thing but doing another:

I have discovered this principle of life — that when I want to do what is right, I inevitably do what is wrong... Oh, what a miserable person I am! Who will free me from this life that is dominated by sin and death? Thank God! The answer is in Jesus Christ our Lord (Romans 7:21, 24–25).

Yes, we *should* love others. I am not exaggerating when I say love is essential to the success of the human race. But the key to loving others, as Paul points out, is not to focus on loving others but to focus on Jesus. It's to understand his love toward us and toward those around us.

We love because God loved us first (see 1 John 4:19). Now that we understand and believe his amazing, unconditional love, we are free to love like never before. No strings attached. No conditions. No undertones of manipulation or insecurity.

I'm sure in the near future, I'll get distracted from my fixation on bacon and bananas and find a new passion. And Chelsea will roll her eyes again when I tell her that it is going to change her life. But there's one thing I'll never take my eyes off: the love of Jesus.

It's the best obsession ever.

- Have you ever tried to do what is right but ended up doing what is wrong? How did that make you feel? What does this tell you about the effectiveness of human effort?

- What are some practical ways you could focus on Jesus' love?

- How does focusing on Jesus help us love others better? How is Jesus' love better than our love?

Day 3: Generosity Looks Like Jesus

You only have to watch the news for about thirty seconds before you are reminded of the need for generosity in this world. Tsunamis, wars, famines, forest fires — everywhere you turn, people are in need.

What really encourages me is how popular generosity is in our culture. Individuals, families, businesses, and even large corporations are finding ways to give back to society. Chances are, you've also participated in some act of generosity recently: donating to relief efforts after a natural disaster, giving a bit extra at the grocery store to fight leukemia, buying a coat to give to a local clothing drive, giving to your church, or volunteering at a soup kitchen. Few things are as exciting and moving as watching true generosity in action. And few things are as close to the heart of God.

God is the original giver. He invented generosity, and generosity is one of the clearest and purest expressions of a heart that follows God. Not that you have to be a Jesus-follower to be generous, of course. I am convinced that generosity is a built-in characteristic of the human spirit, and God was the one who built it in.

Ironically, I think it's often harder to love and give to people who are close to us than to love and give to people who are far away. At least for me, it's relatively easy to feel compassion for people I've never met. I can pray for people, cry for people, and give to people whom I will never know or interact with on a personal level.

Maybe that's why it's easy.

Donating to causes, projects, and needs around the world is awesome, and I highly recommend it. But we sell generosity a little short when we limit it to digging wells or feeding the poor on the other side of the world.

We have an opportunity to be generous in *every* human interaction by giving love, praise, acceptance, and forgiveness. In my opinion, this is the greatest generosity of all, because it is where the greatest risk exists.

These are the people who, sooner or later, will let us down. They will take us for granted. They will abuse our generosity. Will we continue to give freely and with no strings attached, even when our gift is not valued? When our love is not reciprocated?

That's what Jesus did. If you want to understand generosity, consider this: generosity looks like Jesus. He is the greatest giver in the history of the world. John records these words from Jesus:

This is my commandment: Love each other in the same way I have loved you. There is no greater love than to lay down one's life for one's friends (John 15:12–13).

Jesus gave his life to rescue people who would reject him, hate him, use him, and mock him. He doesn't put conditions on his gift. He doesn't ask for it back when people are ungrateful or uninterested. He doesn't get his feelings hurt when he is ignored.

I don't know about you, but I want to love like Jesus. I want to give like Jesus. I want to have such an overflow of life and goodness and love spilling out of me that everyone I come into contact with is changed.

The best source for this generosity is not self-effort. It's not gritting our teeth and forcing ourselves to be nice to nasty people. That might work for a bit, but ultimately self-effort will fail us.

The best source is Jesus. After all, who knows more about generosity than the original giver himself? All it takes is spending a little time with Jesus, and you'll find generosity growing so fast in your life it might scare you.

Remember Zacchaeus in Luke 19? He was a tax collector and a thief, but after he spent a couple hours with Jesus, he became the biggest philanthropist around.

Jesus is the ultimate source of all we have. He invites us to simply open our hearts and let his love for others flow through us.

Now that's generosity.

- What are some of the reasons why people are generous? Are some of these reasons better than others? Why?

- According to John 15:12–13, what is the greatest demonstration of love possible? What does Jesus' sacrifice tell us about his love for us?

- Does understanding Jesus' generosity motivate you to be more generous? How is Jesus' love the best motivator possible for generosity?

Day 4: Aladdin Goes to Church

I'm sure you've heard the story of Aladdin. I am informed it existed long before Disney, but because reading is not my forte, my first real memory of the whole genie-in-a-lamp concept came through the animated version.

In case neither reading nor cartoon-watching are your forte, the story of Aladdin revolves around a poor boy who finds a golden lamp. He happens to rub it, and out squeezes a magical being called a genie who, in return for his freedom, agrees to grant Aladdin three wishes.

Maybe you've thought about using one of your wishes to ask for more wishes. The creators of the Disney version took that into account. Robin Williams, who masterfully voices the genie, says, "Three wishes, to be exact. And *ixnay* on the wishing for more wishes." Based on my vast linguistic abilities, I happen to know that *ixnay* is Pig Latin for "nix." In other words, Aladdin couldn't wish for more wishes.

But as someone recently pointed out to me, he could have wished for more genies.

Problem solved.

That's the power of multiplication. Sure, one genie can only accomplish three things. But imagine what an entire community of genies committed to our well-being could do.

It's safe to say none of us will ever get the chance to find out. You can polish every lamp in IKEA, and I promise, no genies will appear. Security guards probably will, and maybe a psychologist or two, but no genies.

But what we *can* experience is the magic of a community of actual human beings where everyone is committed to our well-being. Not quite as spectacular, maybe, but no less astounding.

That's how family is supposed to work. It's how church is supposed to work. It's how friendships are supposed to work. In general, community remains one of the most powerful forces for good in society.

There is no one person who can provide all that we need. And we can't provide all that is needed for any one person. But we can all contribute with our individual gifts and talents, and ultimately, "the whole is greater than the sum of its parts."

No big deal, but I just quoted Aristotle.

Maybe I'm biased because I'm a pastor, but I'm convinced that the absolute best communities are those that are centered around Jesus. The church is the most obvious example, but in reality Jesus can be at the center of just about any social structure, including our families and our friendships.

That doesn't mean we talk about God and tell Bible stories and sing hymns all the time, of course. Some of the best times I've had with friends have not been religious in the slightest. But they are authentic. They are based on trust. And, ultimately, they are the result of each of us having a relationship with Jesus.

A Jesus-centered community is what happens when a few Jesus-centered people spend time together. That's what the very first church looked like. Luke writes in the book of Acts:

> All the believers met together in one place and shared every-thing they had. They sold their property and possessions and shared the money with those in need. They worshiped together at the Temple each day, met in homes for the Lord's Supper, and shared their meals with great joy and generos-ity — all the while praising God and enjoying the goodwill of all the people. And each day the Lord added to their fellow-ship those who were being saved (Acts 2:44–47).

The best kind of unity comes not from forcing people to act the same and believe the same but from encouraging people to follow a common goal: in this case, Jesus. The closer we get to Jesus, the closer we get to each other. And the more we become like Jesus, the more supportive, loving, and effective our commu-nities will be.

So, here's the call to action: don't wait for the perfect com-munity. My dad used to always say that if a perfect community did exist, as soon as you or I joined it, it wouldn't be perfect any-more, because none of us is perfect. It's far better to belong to a community that loves Jesus — a community that is committed to knowing Jesus, preaching Jesus, and following Jesus.

That's better than a genie in a lamp any day.

- What is the hardest part for you about being part of a community? What is the best part?

- What communities are you a part of — family, church, neighborhood, circles of friends? How do these communities help you? How do you help them?

- Why do you think the church in Acts 2 experienced things like joy, generosity, the goodwill of the people, and growth?

- How does making Jesus the center of our lives make us better members of every community we belong to?

Day 5: It's Where You Belong

Many ancient cultures had rites of passage for young people. These rites included things like trekking across the wilderness with no food, enduring physical wounds that left permanent scars, and killing lions with nothing but a spear.

We have junior high. I'm not sure which is worse.

Junior high is a giant social experiment where hundreds of kids in completely different stages of emotional and physical maturity are thrown together and left to survive however they can. It's like *Lord of the Flies,* only there is homework. And selfies.

I have been out of junior high for longer than I like to admit, but I have vivid memories of the melodrama, the agony, and the angst of that time. Most of it revolved around one thing: fitting in. It was about belonging, about being accepted, about finding where you fit. Having close, loyal friends was the most important thing in the world.

I survived the rite of passage and made it to adulthood. But just because I grew up doesn't mean my need for acceptance went away. Humans have an innate need to belong, to be accepted. Maybe there are a few born hermits out there, but most of us depend on others a lot — probably more than we realize. We need to belong somewhere. We thrive best when we sense that we are in a secure place, a safe place — *our* place.

There is something about love that sets us free to be whom we are meant to be. And that's a good thing. That's how God created us. We are social beings, and he built us to give and receive love continually.

The problem is that as humans, our love is often conditional. We accept people because of what they do for us. Their behavior determines their belonging.

That's not how God works, though. With God, our belonging doesn't depend on our behavior or even our beliefs. God loves us exactly as we are, right now, with no strings attached.

That doesn't mean he approves of every single thing we do or think. But he does approve of *us* as people. That's huge.

It might be tempting to think that if God accepts us unconditionally, we will never change. We will remain in our mistakes and our sin because we won't be motivated to change. Actually, the opposite is true. When we realize how accepted and welcomed we are, we find ourselves wanting to live the way we should. God's love is the greatest motivator possible. It helps us grow more than rules and religion and requirements ever could.

God's acceptance creates a safe place for us to become the people he knows we are capable of becoming. And in that safe place, his grace is present to empower us to change. True transformation always takes place in the context of grace.

The apostle Paul understood this concept well, because he was living proof that it worked. Here is how he described what happened when he met Jesus:

> The grace of our Lord was poured out on me abundantly, along with the faith and love that are in Christ Jesus. Here is a trustworthy saying that deserves full acceptance: Christ Jesus came into the world to save sinners — of whom I am the worst. But for that very reason I was shown mercy so that in me, the worst of sinners, Christ Jesus might display his unlimited patience as an example for those who would believe on him and receive eternal life (1 Timothy 1:14–16 NIV).

Remember, before Paul met Jesus, he was the fiercest, cruelest persecutor of Christians you would find anywhere. He was responsible for mistreating, imprisoning, and even killing people whose only "crime" was loving and following Jesus. Then Jesus knocked him off his donkey, so to speak, and revealed the depth of God's love. It changed everything.

Let's take this concept one step further. Assuming we understand and believe that God loves us first, before we earn his love or prove our worth, then how should we treat others? I think the answer is clear: we should accept them unconditionally as well.

Actually, this principle of belonging before behaving is a defining characteristic of the church. The church is a place where hurting, broken, bad, messed-up people can belong long before their behavior measures up to God's standard. After all, God's standard is perfection, so if we are waiting for that, the church is going to be totally empty all the time.

When we accept people unconditionally — when we welcome and embrace them just as they are — we set them free to change. We provide the perfect environment for them to develop into the best possible version of themselves.

We can't change anyone; only God can. So, our role as the church is to point people to Jesus and to love them unconditionally, whether they change as fast as we'd like or not. That's what God did for us. And at some point in our lives, other human beings did that for us as well.

Now it's our turn.

- What does it mean to accept and love someone unconditionally? Is that hard to do? Why or why not?

- How is Paul's life an example of the power of God's acceptance?

- In your own life, who has shown you acceptance? How did that help you?

- Who in your life could benefit from your unconditional love and acceptance?

LIFE IS to trust God

Welcome

Welcome to session three of *Life Is* _____. This week, you will explore with your group how "life is ... to trust God."

It's easy to trust God when things are going smoothly in life, but what about when you face challenges, trials, and tragedies? At moments like those, it's tempting to think in terms of what you deserve — or think you deserve. *I'm a good person. I don't deserve this.*

But that is a complicated and frustrating way to live. It's a dead-end street.

Living a fulfilled, happy, satisfied life comes from relating to God based not on what you think you earn or deserve but solely on his goodness. On his love. On his generosity.

To begin today's session, get into groups of two or three and answer the following questions together:

- Have you ever felt disappointed in God? Describe the situation.
- As you look back on the situation, did God really let you down? How has your perspective changed?

- How does what you learned in the past about God help you face challenges today?

Video Teaching

The following are a few key thoughts to note as you watch session three of the video. Use the space provided to jot down personal observations or applications.

Sometimes life feels like it's about trusting ourselves and taking care of ourselves. But true life is found in trusting God. It is about trusting in who he is — his faithfulness, supply, power, and strength in our lives.

In Matthew 20:1–16, Jesus describes God's kingdom culture. It's a lesson about trusting God to give us what is right rather than living based on what we think we deserve. What we really deserve is punishment, death, and separation. It's far better to relate to God based on his goodness.

When we simply trust God and his goodness, we discover the spontaneity, adventure, and joy of life.

Life isn't made up of what we've earned or deserve. It's not about whether we've been good enough or prayed enough or done enough for God. It's about relationship with a good, generous God who gives us more than we could ever deserve.

Do we trust that what God gives us is good and right? He's a good God, and what comes from his hands is good.

A lifestyle of trust sets us free. We don't have to keep track of what we deserve. We don't have to compare ourselves to others. We can live in gratitude and joy, knowing God will take care of us.

Group Discussion

Take a few moments to discuss the following questions with your group.

1. Have you ever felt like God or life was giving you something you didn't deserve, whether good or bad? In reality, what do you deserve?

2. In the parable Jesus told in Matthew 20:1–16, why did the first group get upset when they were paid exactly what they had agreed upon with the owner? Can you relate to their feelings?

   Why does their treatment seem unfair? Is it *actually* unfair?

3. Why is relating to God based on what we earn or deserve a dead-end street?

4. How does learning to trust that what God gives us is good and right set us free to enjoy life more?

5. Have you ever compared your lot in life with someone else's? How does that make you feel? Why is that an unwise way to live?

6. Do you truly trust God? Do you believe he is good and that he gives you good things? Why is that sometimes hard to believe?

7. Would you rather live a life of gratitude and joy or a life of trying to get what you deserve? Why? Which do you think makes you a better person to be around?

Closing Prayer

Close your time together in prayer. Here are a few ideas of what you could pray about based on the topic of this session:

- Pray that you will relate to God based on his love, not on your efforts.
- Pray that you will be able to trust God completely, no matter what you might be facing.
- Pray that you will have grace to face difficulties and challenges with faith in God's goodness.
- Pray that you will enjoy your relationship with God more and more each day.
- Pray that you will fulfill God's calling on your life, not from a sense of obligation but from a sense of joy and gratitude.

Weekly Challenge

This week, find a moment to sit down and evaluate what we've discussed today and how you are applying it to your life.

One good way to do this is to write down your three biggest challenges. They might be financial, relational, emotional, physical, or spiritual. Next, write down your three biggest blessings. Be as specific as possible.

Biggest Challenges

1.

2.

3.

Biggest Blessings

1.

2.

3.

Conclude by asking yourself these questions:

- *How am I processing these challenges emotionally? Am I taking them to God or am I trying to carry them on my own?*
- *Do I blame God for these things? Do I look at him as the problem or as the solution?*
- *In light of the blessings and goodness God has shown me, what can I assume about the challenges I'm facing?*

Recommended Reading

Review chapters 5–8 in the book *Life Is* ____. Use the space provided to write any key points or questions you want to bring to the next group meeting.

Between-Sessions Personal Study

Day 1: Jesus Is Fun

Chelsea and I have a motto that we apply to just about everything: if something isn't fun, we aren't going to keep doing it.

Does that sound unspiritual? Selfish? Carnal? If so, let me explain.

First of all, I'm using the word *fun* on purpose. I could have said *have joy* or *experience peace* or something more biblical sounding, and no one would disagree. But there is something about the concept of having fun that catches us by surprise.

And yet, you could make a good argument that Jesus had more fun than just about anyone. Kids and young people liked to hang out with him — which says a lot right there. His teachings and parables often had humorous twists, especially when taken in their cultural context. Hebrews 1:9 says about him, "Your God has anointed you, pouring out the oil of joy on you more than on anyone else." Beyond doubt, Jesus knew how to have fun.

If Jesus had fun, shouldn't we? Shouldn't that be just as high on our priority list as holiness, faith, wisdom, love, and other biblical qualities? For Christians, having fun shouldn't be optional. It should be our default.

Just to be clear, when I say *fun*, I'm not talking about doing dumb, self-destructive things. I'm not talking about going out and getting wasted. I'm not talking about doing anything the Bible calls sin. Here's another good motto to live by: if it's not fun in the morning, it's not fun now.

But just because we avoid sin doesn't mean we don't enjoy

life. Actually, it's the exact opposite. Knowing Jesus frees us to truly enjoy life more.

Why? We have confidence instead of guilt. We live in peace instead of stressing out over everything. Fears don't paralyze us anymore. We don't have to deal with as many harmful consequences of sin. I could keep going, but you get the point. Life with Jesus is more enjoyable all around.

I think the problem is that we take ourselves too seriously sometimes. More specifically, we take our obstacles, our weaknesses, and our responsibilities too seriously.

Yes, those things are important. But Jesus is greater than all of them. Jesus is bigger than our sins, bigger than our issues, bigger than our worries. He knows the past, present, and future, and he loves us regardless of all that. He promised to be with us in every moment. Even death can't separate us from him.

Literally, we have nothing to worry about. Sure, we have to be wise and responsible. I think we all understand that. But sometimes in the name of wisdom we become downright pessimistic, and in our well-intentioned attempts to be responsible, we become controlled by fear.

Our ability to enjoy life is directly related to our ability to trust Jesus. When we truly know God and believe his love for us, we are free to be the happiest people on the planet. We will smile more, laugh louder, and look younger than anyone around us.

Wanting to have fun is not unspiritual. It's a natural part of being human. God created us with the capacity for pleasure, enjoyment, and fun, and he loves to see us happy.

I'm convinced that happiness and holiness are intrinsically connected. The closer we get to Jesus, the more we will enjoy life and the more our lives will look like his. Holiness helps us be happy, and happiness helps us be holy. We don't have to choose one or the other — we get both.

Jesus is fun. Jesus fills my life. Therefore my life is fun. That about sums it up.

- Who created our ability to have fun? What does that say about God's plan for our lives?

- Are specific areas of fear, worry, or doubt in your life keeping you from enjoying God and enjoying life? If so, what are they? What happens to those things when you begin thinking about Jesus' love, presence, and power in your life?

- Hebrews 1:9 says Jesus was anointed with the "oil of joy." What does that mean? Do you think God wants to give each of us that same joy?

- How does enjoying life help us be better examples of God's love to people who don't know him?

Day 2: Who's in Your Boat?

In case you aren't familiar with our city of Seattle, it has a lot of bodies of water. The Puget Sound, which is a long arm of the ocean, goes right alongside it, and there are rivers and lakes everywhere. So, a while back, I had the genius idea of buying a boat.

Now, I am not — nor will I ever be — a sailor or a boater. I don't like being in the ocean, I don't like sand in general, I don't understand tides ... you get the idea. So when I say "genius" idea, I use the term sarcastically.

I found a boat on Craigslist. I should have been suspicious because it only cost 250 dollars. I also bought a vintage motor somewhere — which just means it was really old. It turns out the boat was a rowboat and had no mount for a motor, which should have been a clue that this was not going to work out well, but I was as stubborn as I was oblivious. My friend Elijah and I got the motor attached to the boat, and together with our too-trusting wives, we headed out in the Puget Sound.

The boat was rated for 380 pounds. I won't disclose the combined weight of the four grown adults in our party, but it was definitely more than that. As we moved out, we looked over the edge — one at a time, so we wouldn't tip over — and saw we were literally four inches from capsizing.

Undeterred, I cranked up the motor. I was expecting a satisfying, manly roar: you know, *vroooom*. What I got was more of an anemic mosquito: *bzzzzzzz*.

Maybe half an hour later, we had chugged 600 yards out from shore. That's when a giant ferry crossed our bow. Or maybe it's called the stern. Anyway, our toy boat was four inches out of the water, and these were genuine waves.

I started screaming, "Waves! Waves! Dear God, those are waves!" Others in the boat were using more explicit language, if I recall correctly, but I was crying out to God. That's why I'm the pastor. Meanwhile, people on board the ferry were staring and pointing and — God have mercy on their souls — laughing.

Somehow, we survived. Safe to say, that was the boat's maiden voyage and also its final voyage, at least on the Puget Sound.

That experience is the closest I can come to understanding the panic the disciples felt one day when they were stuck on a boat in the middle of maybe the biggest storm they had ever faced. These weren't newbies, like us — they were professional, experienced fisherman. If they were scared, you know the situation was bad. And oddly, Jesus was sound asleep right when they needed him most.

Luke describes it like this:

As they sailed across, Jesus settled down for a nap. But soon a fierce storm came down on the lake. The boat was filling with water, and they were in real danger. The disciples went and woke him up, shouting, "Master, Master, we're going to drown!" When Jesus woke up, he rebuked the wind and the raging waves. Suddenly the storm stopped and all was calm (Luke 8:23–24).

The point of this story is not the size of the waves or the size of the storm. It's not how sea-hardy the disciples were or how sea-worthy their boat was. The point is that Jesus was in their boat.

When it comes to life, storms are a regular occurrence. It doesn't matter how holy we are or are not — life has a way of sending winds and waves that threaten to swamp us. We often feel four inches from sinking, four inches from failure.

In these moments, it is tempting to look at the size of the

storm. It is tempting to look at our weakness and inability. But what we really need to do is look at Jesus.

Jesus is bigger than any storm. He is the creator of the universe, and there is no way his creation can overwhelm him. In comparison to Jesus, all waves are ripples, all hurricanes are ocean breezes, and all seas are kiddie pools.

I don't know about you, but I can't imagine Jesus waking up and screaming, "Waves! Dear God, what are we going to do?" If Jesus is in your life, you can be sure that he will get you to the other side: the other side of the financial problem, the other side of the business venture, the other side of the relationship conflict, the other side of the health emergency. Jesus will see you through.

I wish I could tell you that you will never experience storms. I wish I could tell you that you will never get wet, that you will never be hurt by the wind and waves. Life can seem impossibly hard at times. Tragedies, loss, and failure are part of the human condition. We've all faced them. But we don't have to face them alone.

Is Jesus in your boat? Then you have nothing to worry about. Sooner or later it will be smooth sailing. You'll find yourself at the other side. You might not even know how you got there, but you'll know one thing for sure: Jesus is with you.

- Have you ever felt like you were sinking in one of life's storms? How did you respond? Looking back, how can you see God at work?

- What do you think Jesus wanted his disciples to learn about handling difficult moments?

- How does knowing Jesus is with you help you face life's storms?

Day 3: Winning the Super Bowl

(*Disclaimer: If you're a Broncos fan, you might want to hashtag this story #toosoon and skip ahead. Don't say I didn't warn you.*)

I'm a big sports fan, and I love football in particular. So one of the sports highlights of my life was when our team — the Seattle Seahawks — won Super Bowl XLVIII.

We didn't just win the Super Bowl, though. We *crushed* the opposing team, the Denver Broncos, 43–8. We scored our first points twelve seconds into the game, and it only got better from there. I have friends in Denver, and you better believe I was texting them mercilessly throughout the game. Yes, I probably need counseling. But it was so much fun.

Two weeks before, we had played our archrivals, the San Francisco 49ers. That was anything but easy. The outcome was up in the air until the very end, when Seattle intercepted a last-minute end zone pass to clinch the win. During that game, we were on the edges of our seats the whole time. No one knew who would win.

But against Denver? Sorry to rub it in (actually, I'm not), but after we returned the second-half kickoff for an 87-yard touch-down, we realized this wasn't even a competition. We were going to win. The outcome was sure.

Celebrations started. Random strangers hugged each other all over our city. As touchdown piled on top of touchdown, we relaxed and reveled in the glory. And continued to text our poor Broncos friends.

If you aren't a sports fan, you're probably rolling your eyes by now. So I'll get to the point. When you know you're going to win, you can relax. You can enjoy the experience. But if the outcome is in doubt, you're on the edge of your seat. You're stressed and tense.

I realize the metaphor breaks down a bit because in football I'm just a spectator, while in life I'm a player. But I would argue that the players themselves were able to relax a lot more when the victory was sure. That doesn't mean they quit doing their job, of course. Rather, their confidence and peace made them more effective players than ever.

The same goes for life. Stress and fear have a way of inter-fering with our game. But when we realize that victory is sure, we not only have more fun in life but we also perform better. We can throw ourselves into life with all our heart and soul, because we understand that our performance cannot jeopardize our vic-tory — it will only contribute to it. Our mistakes aren't going to mess everything up. Just read the end of the book. Jesus wins.

That doesn't mean we drop the ball and walk off the field. We have a part to play in this victory. It's hard work at times, but it's work that takes place within a context of rest, relaxation, and enjoyment because we know who Jesus is. The writer of Hebrews describes our sense of victory this way:

Therefore, since we are surrounded by such a huge crowd of witnesses to the life of faith, let us strip off every weight that slows us down, especially the sin that so easily trips us up. And let us run with endurance the race God has set before us. We do this by keeping our eyes on Jesus, the champion who initiates and perfects our faith (Hebrews 12:1–2).

In other words, because Jesus goes before us, we don't have to worry about the outcome. We are free to run our race and play our game knowing that victory is ours. And as we look to Jesus, we find the strength to leave behind sin and run with endurance.

The reason we win is not because we are so amazing and awesome and skilled. It's because Jesus is. One of the biggest keys to restful living is understanding his role versus our role. If we see ourselves as the star players, we have to live on the edge of our seats. We have to stress and strive and worry. But when we realize that the ultimate victory rests with Jesus, we can actually enjoy the part we play.

Our victory doesn't depend on our blood, sweat, and tears. It depends on his. And he already won the game two thousand years ago.

- How do you feel when you are unsure of the outcome of a challenging situation? How do things change when you realize things are going to work out?

- How does knowing who Jesus is make the challenges of life easier to handle?

- What does the writer of Hebrews mean when he says we are to keep our eyes on Jesus?

- Faith is essential in following Jesus, but if we aren't careful, we can end up putting our faith in faith itself. According to Hebrews 12:2, where does our faith come from in the first place? Why is it important to focus more on Jesus than on our faith?

Day 4: Sack Lunch

Remember the story of Jesus feeding the five thousand? If you've been around church for a while, you've probably heard it. It's found in all four Gospels, probably because it made such a huge impact on the disciples and the crowds. John sets the scene this way:

Jesus soon saw a huge crowd of people coming to look for him. Turning to Philip, he asked, "Where can we buy bread to feed all these people?" He was testing Philip, for he already knew what he was going to do.

Philip replied, "Even if we worked for months, we wouldn't have enough money to feed them!"

Then Andrew, Simon Peter's brother, spoke up. "There's a young boy here with five barley loaves and two fish. But what good is that with this huge crowd?" (John 6:5–9).

Later, we read there were five thousand *men* there — in other words, five thousand families were represented. Jesus, who clearly has a sense for the dramatic, fed them all with the contents of a young boy's sack lunch.

Think about that. God could have fed the crowd by dropping food from heaven. He did that before in the Bible, by the way. But he didn't. He chose to use a specific candidate: a young kid with just an average lunch. The Bible says the contents of his lunch were five barley loaves and two fish. Talk about underwhelming.

Have you ever looked at your gifts and abilities and thought to yourself, *Really, God? How underwhelming is this?* I have. More often than I'd like to admit. I'll be in a social setting somewhere, and suddenly I'll realize I'm agitated and frustrated because everyone around me seems to have an overflow of gifts and abilities, and I don't think I measure up.

Have you ever been with a group of people, and you're happy with your sack lunch, until you discover that the rest of the group seems to have picnic baskets overflowing with fresh fruits and vegetables and cheeses? You have a stained brown paper bag lunch, and you can smell their smorgasbord a mile away. And you're like, "Why, God? Why do I get the sack lunch in life?"

But what you have is perfect. Your gifts and abilities are not a random act of the universe. God planned them for you.

Maybe you are innovative, or creative, or administrative, or artistic. Maybe you can imagine things, organize things, calculate things, say things, hear things, see things, or make things happen. Your gift mix, even if it's five barley loaves and two little fish, was given to you perfectly by the perfect gift giver himself. He knew exactly what he was doing when he designed you. You are complete.

You know what I've determined? I'm just going to enjoy my sack lunch. I'm going to let my five barley loaves and my two little fish work for me. Comparison is a dead-end street. Envying someone else's abilities not only frustrates me but also keeps me from enjoying how God is using my abilities.

When you look at Jesus' miracle in John 6, you realize something. The point isn't the lunch. It isn't how many loaves were there or how big the fish were. The point is *Jesus*. Your gifts and abilities are not an end in themselves. They come from God, they are used by God, and they point to God.

When you find your fullness in the Gift-giver, value the gifts you have, and offer them to God to do whatever he wants — miracles happen. God takes your lunch and feeds multitudes.

And someday, somebody will say, "How did you do what you did in life?"

And you'll reply, "I have no idea. But those barley loaves and those little fish sure went a long way, didn't they?"

- What are your gifts and abilities? In what ways have you wished they were different?

- In what ways do you tend to underestimate or undervalue the person God has made you to be?

- Ultimately, what will bring more peace and satisfaction to your life: the Gift-giver or the gift? Why?

Day 5: Trust Fall

If you've ever been to a youth camp, you've probably been subjected to the psychological torture known as a trust fall. In a typical trust fall, one poor soul is chosen to climb up on a platform and voluntarily fall backward into the (hopefully) waiting arms of his or her teammates. This supposedly encourages team spirit, unity, and trust. I think it encourages nightmares and paranoia, but maybe that's just me.

Now, if you're talking about a bunch of teenage guys catching a teenage girl, things work relatively fine. This is because the girl doesn't weigh that much, and the guys will use any excuse to get a girl in their arms.

At the youth camps I attended, however, I suspect the counselors knew exactly what was going on inside guys' brains. So they tended to avoid picking girls as the victims. Instead, they would pick some large athletic guy. Presumably, this was because he was brave enough to actually do it — and better able to withstand internal injury if the exercise failed.

Now, keep in mind that these trust falls usually took place as part of a whole afternoon of team-building exercises that involved running around the woods in the sun. So, you have this big sweaty kid up above and a whole crowd of skinny sweaty kids down below. Predictably, this often did not end well. I don't remember any actual deaths or paralysis, but the results were never pretty.

Possibly the most sadistic part of the exercise was that the guy who was endangering life and limb had to voluntarily fall. That was really the whole point. He wasn't pushed. He wasn't tricked. He wasn't forced. He had to trust that the others would catch him.

It's debatable whether any of us learned to trust our fellow humans through that exercise. I'm pretty sure some of us learned the opposite, actually.

Why? Because we knew how fallible *we* were. We knew we might not be able to stop that falling, flailing, sweaty human cannonball. We knew that deep inside, we wanted to see what would happen if everyone stepped back and let him hit the ground. Okay, I'm kidding. But the thought did cross our minds.

In real life, trust is an essential part of human interaction. At the same time, most of us have been around long enough to realize humans are not particularly trustworthy. I'm not being pessimistic — I just know my weaknesses, and I know they are common to humanity. Even when we want to be trustworthy, even when we try our hardest to be faithful, we still let each other down at times.

The problem is, because other humans have betrayed our trust, we too easily assume that God will betray it as well. We don't say that, of course. But when we hit a speed bump or a roadblock in life — when we face problems and difficulties and tragedies — it's easy to jump to the conclusion that God is letting us down.

To be honest, I've done this many times. I have no problem trusting God when things are working out in my favor. I tell everyone how good and great and trustworthy God is. But when things take a turn for the worse, I start to wonder if there is anyone down there to catch me.

If our trust only works when it isn't needed, then it isn't really trust. The whole point of trust is to be able to believe the best about someone even when our five senses, our emotions, and our thoughts are screaming otherwise.

In life, unlike summer camp, we don't usually get the choice of jumping off the platform. We often find ourselves in free fall through no action or decision of our own.

However — again, unlike summer camp — someone is always there to catch us. His name is Jesus, and his entire life is proof that he is trustworthy. There could be no greater demonstration of faithfulness than Jesus giving his life for us, even when we were lost and ignorant and antagonistic. It was the single greatest act of faithfulness and generosity in human history.

Now that we are following him, now that we are doing our best to know him and listen to him and love him, is he really going to abandon us? Absolutely not. We can trust him with our lives.

Jesus spent three years with his disciples. He was their mentor, their hero, and their friend. Then the time came for him to do what he came to earth to do. When he told his disciples he was returning to heaven, they didn't just get nervous. They started freaking out. I'm sure they felt confused, hurt, and abandoned.

Jesus told them, "Don't let your hearts be troubled. Trust in God, and trust also in me" (John 14:1). He went on to talk about heaven, about the help of the Holy Spirit, and about the supernatural peace found in him.

I can't predict the ups and downs of life, much less explain them. I can't promise that you will never experience trouble. But I can tell you beyond doubt that God is faithful.

In the words of the beautiful song "Oceans" by Hillsong, "You've never failed, and you won't start now."

• What does the word *trust* mean to you?

• Have you ever been deeply hurt by someone? How did that affect your ability to trust other people or even God?

• Think of a specific time where it was hard for you to trust God. What was the outcome of that experience?

• How do the life and death of Jesus prove that he is trustworthy?

LIFE IS to be at peace with God

Welcome

Welcome to session four of *Life Is* _____. This week, you will explore with your group how "life is ... to be at peace with God."

Have you ever felt like you can't please God? Have you ever wondered if he could really love you? God wants you to be sure of his love and acceptance of you through Jesus. He wants you to know that you are always welcome.

As you begin today, think of a humorous incident where you felt out of place or unwelcome: for example, walking into the wrong public restroom, accidentally interrupting a private meeting, or finding yourself in the middle of an awkward conversation.

Share your stories with the group. Who has the craziest, most awkward, or funniest story?

Video Teaching

The following are a few key thoughts to note as you watch session four of the video. Use the space provided to jot down personal observations or applications.

We discover life when we are at peace with God. The assurance that we are right with him brings us confidence, assurance, and rest.

The story of Mary and Martha in Luke 10 seems counterintuitive. Martha should be the one getting praise because she is the one doing the work. But instead, Mary is praised — for doing nothing but spending time with Jesus.

In this story, Martha represents many of us. We have been taught that we need to work hard and that we get what we deserve. But Jesus shows us a different way.

More important than our work is the principle of our relationship with God. Work isn't bad; but in this moment in the story of Mary and Martha, it wasn't what was needed the most.

When it comes to peace with God, it's not about what we do. We don't have to gain his approval or win his acceptance.

In the midst of a hectic, high-paced lifestyle, it's easy to be anxious and troubled about many things. But there is really only one thing that matters the most, and that is sitting at Jesus' feet.

Jesus is our sufficiency. He is our peace with God. He has done for us what we couldn't do for ourselves.

The things we do for Jesus aren't *for* peace but *from* peace. We are already good with God, and we can do nothing to earn or end that. Now we are free to be with him, to enjoy him, and to follow him.

Group Discussion

Take a few moments to discuss the following questions with your group.

1. Have you ever felt like you can't please God? That he is upset with you and you have to earn his approval? If so, how did that feeling affect your life?

2. Who do you relate to more in the story in Luke 10 — Mary or Martha? Why?

3. What did Jesus appreciate about Mary? What was she doing right?

4. Do you think what Martha was doing was wrong or bad? Why? What was Jesus trying to teach her?

5. How do we have peace with God? What has Jesus done for us to bring us peace?

6. When you feel anxious or troubled like Martha, how does knowing that you have peace with God bring peace to your day-to-day life?

7. What is the difference between working *for* peace and working *from* peace? How does knowing you are already accepted by God help you be free to follow him and do good things?

8. In 2 Corinthians 5:21, Paul writes, "God made him who had no sin to be sin for us" (NIV). What does that mean to you? How does the fact that the righteousness of Jesus belongs to you affect you on a daily basis?

9. Do you enjoy God? Do you enjoy your relationship with him? Why or why not?

Closing Prayer

Close your time together in prayer. Here are a few ideas of what you could pray about based on the topic of this session:

- Pray that you will continue to sense Jesus' love and learn to enjoy his presence.
- Pray that even in the busyness and craziness of life you will have God's peace.
- Pray that you will remember to always cast your cares on Jesus, knowing that he cares for you.

- Pray that you will remember that God welcomes you and accepts you — even when you make mistakes.
- Pray that you will always make Jesus the center of your existence.

Weekly Challenge

Sometime this week, spontaneously drop everything and just spend a few minutes with Jesus. Set aside distractions and worries for a while, put on some soft music, and just focus on Jesus' love for you.

To aid you, pick one or two of the following passages to read and think about. Or, if you have a favorite passage in the Bible, read that instead.

- Psalm 103:1–5, 8–14
- Romans 5:8–11
- Romans 8:31–39
- 1 John 4:7–11, 16–19

This is meant to be a time between just you and God. There is no right or wrong way to do it. Just enjoy God for yourself, by yourself, for a few minutes.

Soon you'll have to head back to "real life," but remember: Jesus is always with you. That same peace and joy you feel when you are alone with him is available to you even in the midst of the craziest circumstances of life.

Recommended Reading

Review chapters 9 and 10 in the book *Life Is* ___. Use the space provided to write any key points or questions you want to bring to the next group meeting.

Between-Sessions Personal Study

Day 1: Why Flies?

When I get to heaven, I have a few questions for God. You probably do too. These are questions like, "How could the universe have been created from nothing?" "Where did you come from?" And, "Why do pain and evil exist?"

High up on my list will be this question: "Why flies?"

I have issues with flies because I have issues with germs. I don't do germs. I can't handle germs. I am obsessed with hand sanitizer because it is my defense against the barrage of germs that life flings at me.

Flies are germ-carrying, microbe-collecting, disease-spreading machines. Everyone knows that. Actually, I have no idea if that's true, but it *feels* true, and that's what matters. Flies crawl on garbage and things I won't mention in print, and then they land on our counters, clothes, food, and skin, happily sharing their germ collection with us. It's disgusting.

Combine my fear of germs with my ability to be distracted by basically anything and you can see why flies are problematic. I might be in the middle of a pastoral meeting, discussing deep matters of theology and philosophy — but if a fly is buzzing around, I can't think of anything else. I watch it everywhere it goes. I wince and flinch at its tiny buzzing presence. I will literally stop the meeting and enlist the support of everyone in the room to send that fly back to the depths of hell from whence it came. And if it happens to land on me, I need to take a shower just to feel human again.

It's amazing how one little insect can make everything seem contaminated, dirty, unclean. In the same way, sin has a way of making us feel contaminated. Keep in mind that *sin* is a Bible word that simply means *mistakes, errors,* or *weaknesses.* It's anything that goes against the good that God has planned for us.

Sin is an unfortunate reality of the human condition. We've all made mistakes. We've all fallen short of perfection. As a result, we've all felt the side effects of guilt, condemnation, and shame.

God never intended us to live in that state, however. That's exactly why Jesus came: to deal with sin and its side effects once and for all. The relief I feel when that fly, with a posse of pastors in pursuit, finally zigzags its way out the window is nothing compared to the peace that Jesus brings. Paul describes it like this:

> Since we have been made right in God's sight by faith, we have peace with God because of what Jesus Christ our Lord has done for us. Because of our faith, Christ has brought us into this place of undeserved privilege where we now stand, and we confidently and joyfully look forward to sharing God's glory.
>
> We can rejoice, too, when we run into problems and trials, for we know that they help us develop endurance. And endurance develops strength of character, and character strengthens our confident hope of salvation. And this hope will not lead to disappointment. For we know how dearly God loves us, because he has given us the Holy Spirit to fill our hearts with his love (Romans 5:1–5).

Peace doesn't mean freedom from all pain or problems. But it does mean pain and problems can't take us down. It means no matter what external struggles we might be facing, we have an inner assurance that everything is going to turn out right in the end.

When we discover peace with God, we discover peace that filters down into every area of life. We find peace despite our mistakes and failures. We find peace in the midst of our difficult situations. We become peaceful people, restful people, beautiful people.

When everything is right with God, everything is right with the world.

- How would you describe peace in your own words?

- Have you ever felt guilt and lack of peace as a result of your mistakes or sins? How did you respond?

- What does Romans 5:1–5 say is the reason we have peace with God? How does that reality help us face — and even benefit from — problems and trials?

- Is there a specific area of your life that is difficult for you to have peace in right now? How can you let God's peace become your peace in that area?

Day 2: Always Never

There are certain words that should never be used in marriage. If you're married, you've probably figured this out; and if you aren't, I'm going to help you out here. These include words like *never*, words like *always*, and words like *fat*. Especially that last one. Unless it's used together with *never*, as in *never fat*. That works. But any other usage of those words is a fatal mistake. I'm telling you this from experience, because I am guilty of using *always* and *never*, and it has never worked out well.

When things get heated in marriage, it's so easy to say things like, "Well, you always say . . ." and "You never do . . ."

This is, of course, an exaggeration, and your spouse typically responds with, "Really? Always? Never? Well, how about when . . ." It only escalates from there.

The problem with these words is they inflict your spouse's past on his or her present and future. You are assuming that based on previous performance, your spouse will *always* act in a particular way. We need to give each other room to grow, to change, and to improve.

As humans, though, this is how we tend to function. We hold people's pasts against them.

That's bad enough. But what if we knew the *future*? What if we knew in advance the bad things people were going to do to us?

I know how I'd react. I'd be mad at certain people right now.

I'd excuse myself from their lives permanently, because I would know that somewhere down the road they are going to betray me or hurt me or offend me.

Here's the crazy thing about God. He knows our past, our present, and our future, yet he still loves us. He still roots for us. He still opens his heart to us. He makes himself vulnerable to betrayal, knowing full well that he *will be* betrayed.

That's crazy. It seems like a waste. Why would God extend his grace and mercy to people he knows will let him down?

If I were God, I'd inflict people's future on them all the time. They'd be happy, just having a great day, doing relatively well in the whole holiness thing, but I would be grumpy. They'd be like, "Why are you so mad at me?"

And I'd say, "Because two years from now, I know exactly what you're going to do. And it ticks me off right now." But that's not God. God loves us regardless of what we did, what we're doing, or what we will do. The fact God loves us today proves he'll love us tomorrow.

I'm not belittling sin. Sin sent Jesus to the cross. Sin steals, kills, and destroys. Sin has negative consequences and, yes, those consequences can affect our future.

But God is a God of second chances. And third chances. And infinite chances. He is quick to forgive, quick to heal, and quick to restore. When he looks at us, he isn't thinking about what we did wrong yesterday or how we're going to mess up tomorrow. He's thinking about how to love us and help us today.

Jesus illustrates this unconditional love throughout the Gospels. Take a look at Matthew 4:23–24:

> Jesus traveled throughout the region of Galilee, teaching in the synagogues and announcing the Good News about the Kingdom. And he healed *every* kind of disease and illness.

News about him spread as far as Syria, and people soon began bringing to him *all* who were sick. And whatever their sickness or disease, or if they were demon possessed or epileptic or paralyzed — he healed them *all* (emphasis added).

Matthew points out that Jesus healed "every kind" of sickness, that people brought him "all who were sick," and that "he healed them all." I'm no statistician, but I'm pretty sure that if Jesus healed 100 percent of the sick people who came, odds are that he healed at least a few people who used their healing to sin more. He must have known that he was healing hands that would steal, eyes that would lust, and mouths that would lie.

But he healed them anyway.

God doesn't hold our mistakes against us, because Jesus' death on the cross took care of every sin — past, present, and future. The peace is permanent. The work is finished. The debt is canceled. Once and for all.

- Why do you think Jesus healed everyone who came to him, not just the "good" people? Is anyone really good enough to deserve healing?

- How does knowing that God loves you despite your weaknesses — past, present, future — affect you today, right now?

- How does Jesus' death on the cross affect the way God treats your sin?

Day 3: The Search

If there's one thing I'm grateful for, it's that I'm not single. I hope it's okay to say that. I've been married fifteen years and counting.

Now, if you're single, there's nothing wrong with that. It's just that for me, what I didn't like about being single was the search. You know what I'm talking about — it's the search for "the one."

I really have nothing to complain about, because I married my first and only girlfriend, Chelsea, whom I had known since we were kids. So I didn't have to search too much. Basically, I lived with my parents, and then I lived with my wife.

The search is all about reading. For instance, you have to read into conversations. He sends you a text message, and you ask your friends to read it. "What do you think this means?" you ask. Or she tells you, "Whoa, your hair is interesting." You think, *Is that because she loves my hair, or because I don't have much hair?*

You also have to read into body language and eye contact. Maybe when you said goodbye she gave you kind of a side hug. Is she saying she's like a sister to you? Or a friend? Or the one for you?

Finally, you have to read minds. You're trying to figure out what he wants or what she needs, and it's impossible and exhilarating and frustrating all at once. Come to think of it, then you get married, and you're still trying to read her mind. But that's beside the point.

Being single and searching for that special someone is not the only season of life we search. In fact, much of life on this planet seems to be a search: for purpose, for significance, for identity, for acceptance, for belonging, for confidence, for satisfaction.

If I could sum it up in a word, I would say we are searching for peace. We are looking for an authentic, permanent, all-encompassing sense that everything is okay. That we are going to make it. That things will work out. Ironically, this search for peace is stressful. Life can be confusing, contradictory, and uncertain, and the tension of trying to make sense of it wears us down.

Life on planet Earth, of course, is broken. Sin entered the human race, and as a result things don't work like they should. So, if you haven't found a spouse yet, it's Adam and Eve's fault. Okay, that might be stretching it. But it was never God's intent for us to experience the desperation, the emptiness, and the constant search for satisfaction that humanity shares.

Here's the problem: a broken world can't heal itself. A fragmented existence can't put itself back together. So the answer to our search cannot be found in this life or on this planet. We have to look outside of our five senses, our logic, our experiences, and our abilities. We have to look to God. He's the only one who can bring true peace to a searching, hurting world.

Jesus said this to his disciples:

"Peace I leave with you; my peace I give to you. Not as the world gives do I give to you. Let not your hearts be troubled, neither let them be afraid" (John 14:27 ESV).

The good news is that this peace is freely and abundantly available in Jesus. We don't have to earn it. We don't have to stress or strive to attain it. We don't have to figure it out. The more we get to know Jesus, the more his peace becomes a defining characteristic of our lives.

Life involves a lot of seeking and searching. But when it comes to peace, the hunt is over. The search is complete. Jesus is our peace.

- What are some things you are searching for in life?

- Do you think it is possible to fill your internal needs for belonging, peace, and satisfaction with external things like money, fame, power, and material possessions? Why or why not?

- How would you describe the peace that Jesus gives? How is this peace different or better than the kinds of peace this world offers?

Day 4: Dancing with Strangers

Have you ever danced with a stranger? I'm not referring to you literally asking a stranger to dance. I mean the unintentional, awkward, comical dance that happens when you nearly run into someone walking the opposite way.

This seems to happen to me often. I blame cellular devices, because now people don't just *walk* anywhere. We walk and talk.

Or maybe we walk and check our email, or reply to text messages, or play games. But the point is: we aren't paying much attention to where we are going.

People call it multitasking, which explains my failure at this process because I am not a multitasker. I am the furthest thing there has ever been from a multitasker. When I'm talking on the phone, I'm the guy who has to go to some secluded corner and pace back and forth until I'm done with my conversation.

The other day I was on my cell phone, probably talking to Chelsea, because communication is important to marriage. I was walking along and building my marriage at the same time. Suddenly, I looked up and this nice gentleman and I almost kissed. Personal space boundaries had been crossed a long time ago, and we were officially way too close.

We were both like, "Whoa, sorry."

I politely dodged to one side, but he did the same. Now we were even closer. Then I went the other way, and of course he did too. After dancing this way for a moment, I lowered my phone and whispered, "Which way are you going to go? Because I'll go the opposite way."

In John 6, which we looked at in an earlier session, Jesus poses essentially this same question to his disciple Philip. The story is a familiar one — Jesus is about to feed thousands of people with the contents of a little boy's sack lunch. Here's how John describes it:

> Jesus soon saw a huge crowd of people coming to look for him. Turning to Philip, he asked, "Where can we buy bread to feed all these people?" He was testing Philip, for he already knew what he was going to do.
>
> Philip replied, "Even if we worked for months, we wouldn't have enough money to feed them!" (John 6:5–7).

What's fascinating to me in this story is that Jesus already knows what he is going to do. His question to Philip is a setup. It's a trick question.

I've heard it said that if God — who knows everything — asks you a question, he isn't looking for information. That's a good thing to keep in mind. Jesus wasn't expecting Philip to be the answer for the needs of all these people. He was asking Philip, "Which way are you going to go? Are you going to try to figure this out on your own? Or are you going to turn to me?"

It's human nature to want to know all the answers and to be the solution to every problem. After all, God is a problem-solver, and he made us in his image. But sooner or later, we are going to face challenges we can't overcome on our own. In that moment, which way are we going to go?

Once we understand the power and the reality of Jesus, the answer gets a lot easier. Just turn to Jesus. He is our source. He is our solution.

It's worth noting that the disciples *did* ultimately participate in the solution. They handed out the bread that Jesus had miraculously provided. Jesus did the hard part — the impossible part, actually — and they had the unforgettable privilege of going along for the ride. They couldn't possibly have predicted how things would work out. And that was exactly Jesus' point.

How can you have peace in impossible circumstances? It's not by figuring out what you are going to do. It's not by knowing all the solutions. It's by turning to Jesus. He is your source and your solution.

- What is your first reaction when you are facing difficult situations? How do you handle any negative emotions that might come up?

- Does Jesus ever get worried about difficult things in your life? Why or why not? How could Jesus' attitude toward your problems help you keep a healthy outlook on life?

- Have you ever been in an impossible situation that somehow worked out better than you could have ever imagined? Looking back, what was God's part in the solution? What was your part?

Day 5: No Crying in Basketball

Many people knew my dad, Wendell Smith, as a great preacher, pastor, and author. His life was a blessing to people around the world. I can speak from personal experience that he was an incredible father, friend, and family man as well.

My dad was also a basketball coach. Most people don't know that, because his career lasted for just one season. He coached my sister's high school varsity team at our local Christian school in Portland, Oregon.

Now, before this story goes any further, I should mention that I have nothing against female athletes. I enjoy women's golf, women's tennis, women's gymnastics, and more. Just for the record.

Dad took over the team with aspirations of really turning around the entire franchise. He expected a victorious, awesome, winning season. That didn't pan out. The team went 1–14, I believe. I was kind of the honorary water boy, and I remember we lost one game 68–8. It was a rough year.

I think Dad felt that because he was a preacher and a leader, he could motivate these young ladies. The problem was he was not prepared to coach girls in this particular stage of life. I remember Dad coming home and saying to my mom, "Gini, I just don't understand. There's so much crying. And they're not even crying about basketball. They're crying about the guy who broke up with them. I just want them to do layups, you know? We're trying to do layup drills, and I've got girls crying. I'm not their counselor. I'm not their confidant or their dad. I'm their coach. There's not supposed to be crying in basketball."

If you've ever had a coach in sports, that makes sense, right? Your coach is not your best friend or your therapist. He or she is there to help you be a top-notch performer — to get more production and efficiency and skill out of you than you yourself thought possible.

Sometimes we treat God like a coach. We think he has a big whistle around his cosmic neck and his main goal is for us to run drills, win games, and fulfill our destinies. God doesn't have time for emotions and tears, we think. There is no crying in life — you get in there and fight, fight, fight. You do what God tells you to do, and nothing matters more than winning.

I've got good news. That's not God. In fact, God would rather you cry on his shoulder than do the layup drills. Why? Because

God's primary purpose for humanity is not destiny or performance or accomplishments. It's relationship.

Yes, God wants you to be successful. Yes, God wants to help you physically, occupationally, financially, and professionally. But first and foremost, he wants you to know him relationally.

God is not obsessed, as so many of us tend to be, with success. With the "American Dream." With a certain balance in our checking account. With image and style and swag. God's primary concern is that we know him and that he knows us.

David describes God's compassion and sympathy toward us this way:

> The LORD is compassionate and merciful, slow to get angry and filled with unfailing love ... The LORD is like a father to his children, tender and compassionate to those who fear him. For he knows how weak we are; he remembers we are only dust (Psalm 103:8, 13–14).

The writer of Hebrews, speaking of Jesus, says this:

> This High Priest of ours understands our weaknesses, for he faced all of the same testings we do, yet he did not sin. So let us come boldly to the throne of our gracious God. There we will receive his mercy, and we will find grace to help us when we need it most (Hebrews 4:15–16).

God is not standing on the sidelines of our lives with a clipboard and stopwatch, yelling at us for messing up yet another play. He is helping us, comforting us, and cheering us on.

Through Jesus, we have peace with God. We relate to him based on love and grace, not our performance. We can approach God confidently because we are fully approved and accepted through Jesus.

So go ahead — cry on his shoulder. God won't be disappointed in you. He won't bench you or cut you from the team. He'll comfort you, accept you, and help you.

- Do you think that God is proud of you? Why or why not?

- In Psalm 103 and Hebrews 4, we read that God knows our weaknesses but doesn't reject us; he shows compassion and provides help instead. How does knowing that help you face your own weaknesses? How does it change the way you pray and relate to God?

- Does knowing that God's primary goal is to develop relationship with you affect the way you live? In what way?

LIFE IS to be at peace with yourself

Welcome

Welcome to session five of *Life Is____*. This week, you will explore with your group how "life is ... to be at peace with yourself."

Have you ever gotten so nervous or distracted about something you had to do — maybe a meeting you had to attend or presentation you had to make — that you couldn't even enjoy the present? We've all been there, probably many times. Fear of tomorrow can steal our satisfaction and fulfillment today.

Today is all we have, though. So how can we learn to trust God and enjoy today? That is the focus of today's session.

Before you get started, get into groups of two or three people. Share with your group an odd or recurring nightmare you have, like your teeth falling out or being caught in public in nothing but your underwear. Alternately, share a phobia you have, such as fear of spiders or cats.

Then compare notes. Who has the funniest or most unlikely nightmare or fear?

Video Teaching

The following are a few key thoughts to note as you watch session five of the video. Use the space provided to jot down personal observations or applications.

In Revelation 1:8, Jesus says that he is "the Alpha and Omega." That means he is the first and last. Genesis 1:1 says something similar: "In the beginning God ..." In other words, God was first. He was before the beginning.

The fact that God is first means he is bigger, he is better, and he is the champion. He has never been second and never will be. He is first whether we recognize it or not.

Because God is first, he is more. No matter what difficulty we might face, God is more than enough to handle it.

TO BE AT PEACE WITH YOURSELF

Peace is about proportion and perspective. When things are blown out of proportion or we lose perspective, we lose peace. But understanding that God is first restores our perspective.

Positive thinking is good, but it isn't enough to bring true, lasting peace. It won't aid us in the deepest parts of our soul. We need God.

Because God is first, he is before. Wherever we're going, God's already been there and already is there. He knows what is going to happen.

Peter's denial of Jesus in Mark 14 illustrates Jesus' foreknowledge. But more than that, it illustrates how Jesus goes before us, even in difficult times, and helps us find victory.

God's foreknowledge meant that if he loves you now, he'll love you tomorrow.

Group Discussion

Take a few moments to discuss the following questions with your group.

1. Do you have any fears about the future? If so, how do those fears affect your level of peace today?

2. What does it mean that Jesus is the "Alpha and Omega"?

3. What are some ways that people try to find peace outside of God? Are these things good or bad? How effective are they?

4. What does the fact that God is *more* mean to you? How does it help you live in peace even when you are facing challenges?

5. Do you think it's possible to find true peace within ourselves, or do we need a source outside ourselves? Why?

6. What does the fact God is *before* mean to you? How does it help you live in peace?

7. How does the fact God loves you now prove he'll love you forever?

Closing Prayer

Close your time together in prayer. Here are a few ideas of what you could pray about based on the topic of this session:

- Pray that you will have an understanding of how powerful and present God is.
- Pray that you will have peace in your current circumstances, whatever those might be.
- Pray that will you have a clear perspective on life, on your challenges, and on God.
- Pray that you will face the future in faith, not in fear.

Weekly Challenge

At some point this week, take time to think back over your life and make a list of some of your most challenging moments. Maybe you've experienced times of illness or tragedy, or maybe you've faced financial obstacles.

Look at your list and answer these questions:

- What were your biggest fears when you were facing those challenges? Did they come true? Was it as bad as you thought it would be?
- In what ways can you look back now and see how God was with you the whole time?
- How are you a better person now because of what you went through?
- How does the knowledge of God's presence help you have peace in your current circumstances and in upcoming challenges?

Recommended Reading

Review chapters 11 and 12 in the book *Life Is* _____. Use the space provided to write any key points or questions you want to bring to the next group meeting.

Between-Sessions Personal Study

Day 1: Who Completes You?

As I mentioned earlier, I've been married to Chelsea for fifteen years and counting. In our marriage, she is without a doubt the better human being.

I used to think marriage consisted of two people who each represented 50 percent coming together and making 100 percent. In other words, I thought that a husband and wife were to complete each other. We were meant to make up what was lacking in each other.

That is true to a certain degree. Spouses tend to divide up responsibilities according to their strengths and weaknesses, and they function as a team. For example, in our marriage, Chelsea handles the bills and the banking and the house and the cooking, while I handle the talking and clothes shopping.

That looks a lot worse on paper than it did in my head. Like I said, she's the better half.

But on an emotional, relational, spiritual level, we both need to be at 100 percent. That is, our security and confidence need to be based on something more than each other. I can't expect Chelsea to make me a complete, whole, healthy person. She's a human just like me. That would be unfair to her and would ultimately sabotage our relationship.

Only God can provide that kind of completeness. And when Chelsea and I each find our security in him, our marriage works better than we could have ever thought possible. We are able to serve and love each other freely. Instead of functioning from deficiency, we function from an overflow of God's approval and grace.

The same principle holds true for other relationships and for life in general. When we find peace in Jesus, we find peace throughout life.

Without Jesus, we are forced to base our sense of value on ourselves: our accomplishments, our talents, our abilities, our successes, our possessions. That only works for so long, because sooner or later our humanity kicks in and we fail. And if our identity is based on our performance, then when we fail, we are failures.

That's not how the gospel works. That's not how grace works. Jesus finds us when we deserve him least but need him most. The best route to self-discovery is Jesus-discovery. Jesus makes life make sense. He gives us purpose, value, and acceptance. His love completes us.

Here is what Paul says about God's love:

> May you have the power to understand, as all God's people should, how wide, how long, how high, and how deep his love is. May you experience the love of Christ, though it is too great to understand fully. Then you will be made complete with all the fullness of life and power that comes from God (Ephesians 3:18–19).

God freely gives us his love. He declares that we are valuable and important not because we are so awesome at life but because he loves us. That's all that really matters.

- Have you ever been in a relationship where the other person wanted more from you than you could give? How did that affect the relationship?

- What are some things that we need to get from God rather than from other people?

- What does it mean to be complete, as Ephesians 3 says? How does understanding God's love make us complete?

- How does finding our security and identity in God help us have successful human relationships?

Day 2: Constants and Variables

I have friends who like math. I used to think they were faking it just to look smart, but they're not. While the rest of us enjoy golf and movies and eating out with friends, these guys get their grins and giggles out of adding, subtracting, solving, and resolving.

They say they like math because it's predictable: they get the same result every time they solve a problem. That's exactly why I *don't* like math: I get a different result every time. Numbers and I don't really get along. But there is something even worse than numbers in math: *letters* in math.

That seems inherently contradictory. Why would you take letters — which were meant to form words and sentences and paragraphs — and make them do the job of numbers? When I was taking algebra, this confused me every time. There would be this string of numbers and symbols all doing their normal math thing, and suddenly I would come across an *n* or an *x*. I would think, *Hey there, little buddies, you're in the wrong class. You must be looking for English Lit down the hall. This is math.*

Worst of all, the letters didn't always mean the same thing. That's probably why they are called *variables*, now that I think about it. They change their value from problem to problem. Sometimes they can have multiple values in the same problem depending on other variables, and the best you can do is make a list of possible answers. How unsatisfying is that?

Life is full of variables, in case you haven't noticed. There are more unknowns than knowns. There are more variables than constants. There are more possible outcomes than we can predict, no matter how smart, educated, or experienced we are.

There is a lot to be said for preparation, foresight, and wisdom. But no matter how hard we try, we can't predict the future, and we certainly can't control it. We can't guarantee our life will be pain-free. We can't promise we will never face trials and tragedy. Life has tough moments, and we all have times when we feel overwhelmed and out of control. Our limitations can cause us to stress out — or they can cause us to depend more than ever on Jesus.

In the midst of an uncertain life, there is one thing that never changes: Jesus. Hebrews 13:8 says he is "the same yesterday, today, and forever." His love for us won't change, his commitment to us won't change, and his ability to protect and provide for us won't change.

Understanding Jesus' constancy gives us peace in an inconstant world. Paul wrote this encouragement to the Philippian church:

> Don't worry about anything; instead, pray about everything. Tell God what you need, and thank him for all he has done. Then you will experience God's peace, which exceeds anything we can understand. His peace will guard your hearts and minds as you live in Christ Jesus (Philippians 4:6–7).

Notice that last phrase: "As you live in Christ Jesus." The key to living in God's peace is to stay connected to Jesus. He is our peace. He is our guarantee that life will work out.

You and I don't know the future — but God does. And he's not stressed about it. If God were worried about tomorrow, pacing the halls of heaven and wiping the sweat from his forehead, that would be our cue to be terrified. But he's not. He knows what the future holds, and he already has plans in place to make even the bad things turn out for our good.

When we rest in the unchanging, immovable love of God through Jesus, we discover a peace that surpasses understanding.

• Have you ever been afraid of what the future held? How did you respond?

- If you could know your own future, do you think you would be less worried or more worried than you are now? Why?

- What are some of the characteristics of Jesus that will never change?

- How does the fact that Jesus never changes help you deal with the constant changes of life?

Day 3: You Don't Care

When it comes to money, my brain doesn't operate in terms of prices, costs, and totals. I don't look at price tags when I shop, for example. They're an afterthought: I check them when I'm already standing in line. And I start to twitch and sweat when I have to deal with budgets.

For that reason, Chelsea handles the finances in our family. It's not a matter of preference, it's a matter of survival.

This is unfair to Chelsea. I admit it. Sometimes she'll be at the table balancing the checkbook or looking at our budget, and

I'll be watching golf on TV. I can tell by her body language and various mutterings that she's not excited about the totals.

So I try to show interest. I really do. But I think I must appear insincere. Maybe it has to do with the fact that I only come over during commercial breaks.

To be really candid, this is where friction can come into our marriage. Chelsea starts to say things like, "Judah, do you even care? Do you care about our financial situation? Are you listening?"

It's not that Chelsea lacks faith or strength. She married me, right? But if I don't care, then she is the only one who cares. She is alone with all the bills and the burdens and the cares, and I'm watching TV or painting pictures in the garage. It's overwhelming.

In session four, we read about Jesus visiting the house of his friends, Mary, Martha, and Lazarus. Look again at the story told in Luke 10:

> Now as they went on their way, Jesus entered a village. And a woman named Martha welcomed him into her house. And she had a sister called Mary, who sat at the Lord's feet and listened to his teaching. But Martha was distracted with much serving. And she went up to him and said, "Lord, do you not care that my sister has left me to serve alone? Tell her then to help me."
>
> But the Lord answered her, "Martha, Martha, you are anxious and troubled about many things, but one thing is necessary. Mary has chosen the good portion, which will not be taken away from her" (Luke 10:38–42 ESV).

Martha is busy. Martha is working hard. Martha is getting things done. They are important things, things that someone has to do. Mary isn't helping. She's just sitting in the living room listening to Jesus. So Martha says to Jesus, "Don't you care?"

I don't think Martha is only frustrated by her sister. I think she feels alone and abandoned. She's asking a bigger question: "Jesus, do my concerns matter to *you*? Are my worries and responsibilities important to *you*?"

Have you ever felt that way about God? We get stressed, anxious, and worried, and we start to think the duties and details of our lives don't matter to God. *God doesn't care about the three cavities that I have to get filled, or that my son just twisted his ankle on the soccer field, or that my little girl's ballerina outfit ripped and I have to rush to the store to buy a new one. God doesn't care, so I have to carry the weight of it all.*

It almost feels selfish to pray about these things. God has the universe to worry about. He has an entire planet to care for. What are my cares and concerns in the face of all that?

It's interesting to me that Jesus didn't correct Martha for working. He didn't belittle her busyness or criticize her concerns. She was doing what she needed to do in that moment, and I think Jesus appreciated it. Instead, he said what her sister was doing was necessary and good, and he wasn't going to tell her to stop. But it wasn't a rebuke. He didn't tell Martha to set down the hummus and pita and come sit at his feet.

I think Jesus' gentle reply was his way of reminding Martha that she wasn't alone. He was there, and he cared for her. He cared for the details, but he cared even more for her as a person.

It sounds great to be Mary all the time, and to just enjoy God's love and revel in his rest. But most of life consists of Martha moments. We have schedules, jobs, obligations, and responsibilities.

God cares about those things more than we realize. He is aware of them; he is thinking about them; and he wants to help us with them. We read in 1 Peter 5:7, "Give all your worries and cares to God, for he cares about you."

Peace doesn't mean abandoning all activity. It doesn't mean building a hut on a mountain somewhere and spending every moment in prayer and Bible reading. It doesn't even mean living stress-free or problem-free. Peace means knowing that no matter how hectic life is, you are not alone. You are not abandoned. You don't have to carry your cares by yourself.

Jesus cares about what you care about, because he cares about you.

- Have you ever felt completely alone in a difficult season? How did you respond? How did you get through that time?

- What challenges or worries are you facing right now? How does knowing that Jesus cares for you help you face those things?

- How can we "give all our worries and cares to God" as 1 Peter 5:7 says?

Day 4: Crazy Busy

Sometimes I sit and remember what life was like without children. Don't get me wrong — I love my children. I'm obsessed with them. They are absolutely the best, second only to my wife. But life with three kids is considerably crazier than when we were first married.

If you have kids, you can relate. Do you remember what it was like when you were first married and you didn't have kids? Every night was date night. You didn't have to schedule it, plan for it, or find a babysitter for it.

Do you remember how when you wanted to go somewhere, you just got in the car and drove off? We all had no idea how easy we had it. Now, Chelsea and I do rock-paper-scissors just to see who has to load our offspring into the car. That's how painful the process is.

"What are you wearing? No, you can't wear pajamas to church. We're the pastors. What are you thinking? Come on, people."

Sometimes it feels like the entire universe in conspiring to keep us from getting into our vehicle. "My shoes hurt." "I forgot to go to the bathroom." "She spilled her juice on me."

Lately, we've been getting this one: "I don't like this shirt. I'm not going to the mall wearing this." And I'm like, "Really? You're seven. Since when do you have an opinion about what you wear?"

By the time you actually get to the mall or church or wherever you're going, you're exhausted. And unloading is just as bad. Strollers. Diaper bags. Snacks. Chasing runaways. Finding diapers that were forgotten in the stroller days earlier.

Then, somewhere along the way, you see a young, perfectly poised couple who clearly do not have kids. They look at you in the throes of your parental chaos, and you know exactly what they are thinking, because it's what you used to think before you had kids. *Wow. You need to pull yourself together. You need to keep your kids in line. You need to . . .*

They have no idea.

Earlier we looked at Luke 10. In this passage, Martha and Mary had a little sibling spat over basically who was going to do the dishes. Here again is how Luke describes the conversation:

Martha was distracted with much serving. And she went up to [Jesus] and said, "Lord, do you not care that my sister has left me to serve alone? Tell her then to help me." But the Lord answered her, "Martha, Martha, you are anxious and troubled about many things" (Luke 10:40–41 ESV).

We have already talked about how God cares about what we care about. But I'd like to make another point from this passage: if we aren't careful, we can let our busyness define us. We can let it control us. We can get so caught up in what we have to do and how much everything depends on us that we forget what is most important.

I think that's where Martha was headed. Jesus wanted to remind her that her identity and value were not based on what she did, but on her relationship with him.

Luke says Martha was *distracted, anxious,* and *troubled.* We've all been there. As we've established, it's a regular occurrence for parents of small kids.

In the midst of the craziness of life, it's easy to get stressed and worried and fearful. It almost seems irresponsible *not* to be that way. After all, we need to foresee danger. We need to plan for adversity. We need to be ready for anything. We need to be wise and responsible. The Bible has a lot to say about all those things.

But Jesus is calling a timeout here. He's asking Martha,

Mary, and all of us to remember what is most important. The answer isn't a job title or a to-do list. It's Jesus.

Relationship with Jesus is the most peaceful, most sustainable way to handle the pressures of life.

- Have you ever met someone who is chronically busy? Have you ever met someone who always seems to be at peace? Who would you rather be around? Why?

- Do you ever find yourself so busy with daily tasks that you can't focus on what is most important? How does focusing on Jesus and your relationship with him simplify things?

- Is the life you live right now sustainable? That is, could you carry on at this pace for the next ten, twenty, thirty years? Are there things you could change to make your life more sustainable?

Day 5: Are We There Yet?

If you've ever gone on a long car ride with kids, you already know the one question that you will hear more than any other: "Are we there yet?"

"Really?" That's what I wish I could say in reply. "Would I still be driving if we were there already?" But I can't say that, because I'm supposed to be the mature one. I'm supposed to be an example for these impressionable kids. So I say "no" for the fifteenth time and keep driving.

Meanwhile, someone spills his juice in the backseat. Someone else thinks she is going to be sick. And no one — absolutely no one — can seem to coordinate bathroom breaks with anyone else in the vehicle.

Sometimes you play games to try to pass the time. You look for license plates from every state, or you score points for wildlife you spot. But ultimately, everyone knows it's just a way to pass the time until you get there — wherever *there* is.

The closer you get to your destination, the more things unravel. The last thirty minutes are pure chaos, because everyone knows they're almost there, and they can't wait to get there. Somehow, all that emotion translates into a lot of noise and fighting.

It's enough to make you pick vacation destinations that are within a thirty-minute radius of your house. Or invest in straitjackets.

Have you ever arrived at a long-awaited, highly anticipated destination only to discover that it was profoundly ordinary? Or even disappointing? Maybe a friend or family member had talked this place up to you, and you were expecting that greatest vacation ever. This was going to be the event your family remembered the rest of their lives. It was going to give you permanent hero status as a parent.

So you pack up the minivan, load up the kids, and overdose on junk food for eight hours, only to be met with mediocrity. Maybe the idyllic cabin in the woods turns out to be a rundown shack with an outhouse. Or the crystalline lake ends up being a swamp with more bugs per square foot than the Amazon jungle.

But you're there now, so you find yourself trying to sell it to the rest of the family. You're like, "Isn't this awesome? Look! A snake! Dirt! Nature! Outdoor plumbing!" They're not buying it. So much for hero status.

Sometimes we treat life like it's all about the destination. We are on a journey somewhere, we think. Maybe it's graduation, or marriage, or kids, or a certain job, or a particular salary figure. Someday we'll get there, and then we'll be happy. Everything will be awesome once we reach our destination.

But "someday" usually turns out to be rather ordinary. The highlights we've anticipated come and go with little fanfare. If that happens too many times, we start to get disillusioned. *Is this all there is to life?* we wonder. *Is the trip even worth it?*

Here's the deal. *Someday* will never make us happy, because we never live in someday. We only live in *today*, and today always feels rather ordinary.

Life is not about the destination. It's about the journey. It's about where we are right now, about what God is doing today. It's about being with Jesus, about knowing Jesus, about doing life with Jesus.

Yes, goals are great. Faith and hope and expectation are a wonderful part of life. Don't get me wrong. But looking forward to the future should never steal our joy from the present.

If you aren't happy now, chances are you'll never be happy. Why? Because right now, right where you are, God is good. Maybe that's hard to see because of all the negative stuff you've had to face. But I promise you, God has been good to you, and he's just getting started.

The prophet Isaiah, speaking about Jesus — who would be born hundreds of years later — wrote this: "Look! The virgin will conceive a child! She will give birth to a son and will call him Immanuel (which means 'God is with us')" (Isaiah 7:14).

In other words, Jesus would be known for being with us. He wouldn't be a God who hid in heaven, aloof from our problems and pain. He would be with us all the time. Some of Jesus' last words to his disciples were: "Be sure of this: I am with you always, even to the end of the age" (Matthew 28:20).

Being at peace with yourself starts by meeting God here, now, just as you are. It comes from realizing that God is with you and will never leave you. He is on your side; he is for you; and he will see you through whatever bad things you're facing.

Don't wait for *someday* before you allow God's peace and joy into your life. Start now. His goodness and greatness and grace aren't far off. They are available for you right where you are.

Life is a journey, and Jesus promises to be with you the entire way. He's the ultimate travel companion. So enjoy the journey, and the destinations will take care of themselves.

- Do you tend to enjoy life right now, or are you always looking forward to the future? Why do you think that is?

- What are some destinations or goals you are looking forward to? What do you need to do to enjoy the journey right now?

- How does understanding who God is make life more enjoyable? What are your favorite things about life with God?

LIFE IS to enjoy God

Welcome

Welcome to session six of *Life Is*____. This week, you will explore with your group how "life is ... to enjoy God."

The first step in enjoying God is to realize how much he enjoys you. God doesn't just put up with you or tolerate you — he truly enjoys you. He looks forward to spending time with you, listening to you, and living life with you.

If you have kids, you probably understand this already. Long before they could reciprocate your feelings, you already loved them. Do you remember watching them sleep? Even if the day had been hectic and they had not been on their best behavior, when you looked down on their peaceful faces, you felt an overwhelming love for them. That's how God feels toward us all the time.

God is not nearly as worried about our weaknesses as we sometimes think. Not that he takes sin lightly, because anything that hurts us hurts him. But he wants to take the stress out of our mistakes. It's not about performance. It's about love.

As you begin today, share with the group a time when you embarrassed your parents, or your kids embarrassed you, in public. Do you laugh about it together now?

Video Teaching

The following are a few key thoughts to note as you watch session six of the video. Use the space provided to jot down personal observations or applications.

Much of our satisfaction in life comes from learning to truly enjoy God, and that starts with us believing he enjoys us.

No matter how petty or insignificant something might be, if it's a big deal to us, it's a big deal to God. He listens to us because he loves us and enjoys being with us.

The story of Jesus healing the lame man in John 5:1–15 is a picture of the chaotic, dog-eat-dog society we live in. Sometimes we think the only way to get ahead is to be better, stronger, and faster than everyone. It's a stressful way to live, but Jesus offers a better way.

Jesus introduced an entirely new world to this man. He simply told him to get up and walk. The man didn't understand who Jesus was or how he would be healed, but he was healed anyway.

Jesus wanted the man to know that the consequences of sin were even worse than physical illness, but the answer was Jesus himself.

Jesus offers us a new way of existing. We can rest in him. We can enjoy him and enjoy life. He will take care of us.

In Matthew 11:28–30, Jesus describes this new life. He has a course and a plan for us, but his burden is light. It is doable. It is enjoyable.

We get to live as Jesus-followers, and our lives are characterized by righteousness, peace, and joy.

Group Discussion

Take a few moments to discuss the following questions with your group.

1. Is it hard for you to believe God really enjoys being with you or cares about the details of your life? Why?

2. Have you ever felt like life belongs to whoever is first, fastest, or most manipulative? Is that an enjoyable way to live?

3. What areas of life are most stressful for you? How does knowing God enjoys you help you enjoy life?

4. How does Jesus deal with the problem of sin in our lives? How does this set us free to enjoy life more?

5. If we truly believe God is in control of the heavens and earth, how should we face the needs and cares of day-to-day life?

6. What does Jesus say in Matthew 11:28–30 about our lifestyle when we follow him? Are you experiencing this? Why or why not?

Closing Prayer

Close your time together in prayer. Here are a few ideas of what you could pray about based on the topic of this session:

- Pray that you will know beyond a doubt that God enjoys you and is proud of you.
- Pray that you will truly enjoy life with God and that it will be more about his love for you than what you do for him.
- Pray that you will trust God and rely on him for everything — from the smallest details to the greatest challenges.
- Pray that you will experience the righteousness, peace, and joy of life with Jesus.
- Pray that you will fall more and more in love with Jesus for the rest of your life.

As You Move Forward

This is the conclusion of this study, but in reality it is only the beginning. God can't wait to live life with you. He has amazing plans for you — plans to bless you, to prosper you, to protect you, and to help you.

Maybe in the past you've been hesitant to trust God completely. Maybe life has been tough and you wonder if he is trustworthy. Or maybe you've been burned by religion or hurt by religious people. Those things are real, and they are painful. But they don't have to define your walk with God. His love for you is selfless and permanent. It has no strings attached.

This is the perfect time to make a commitment to God. Not by vowing to be perfect or to try harder or to pray more, but simply by letting him love you. By realizing that he is there for you in every circumstance, in every success and failure, in every tragedy and triumph.

As you follow Jesus, you will discover happiness, fulfillment, and satisfaction. You will discover that life is complete in God. You were meant to be with him, and you will be happiest when you discover yourself in him.

Remember that at any moment you can talk to God. That's all that prayer is. God is always listening, and he will help you in ways you could never imagine.

The Bible is God's love letter to humanity. It's a big book, and parts of it can be confusing at first. Don't worry. The more you read it, the more the pieces will come together and start to make sense. If you've never read it before, a great place to start is the Gospels — Matthew, Mark, Luke, and John. They are simply stories about Jesus' life, teachings, and love for us.

Hopefully, this group has been a safe place for you to draw closer to God. That's what the church is for: to be a family, a home, and a community where people can help one another. So, as you conclude this time, look for ways to build real relationships with those who are on this same journey of following Jesus. Going to church or attending groups like this one are an easy way to do that, and you'll discover lifelong friends who will be there when you need them most.

Life is all about Jesus and his love for you. Can you think of anything more amazing than that?

Recommended Reading

Review chapters 13–16 in the book *Life Is* _____. Use the space provided to write any key points or questions you want to discuss with a friend or family member in the coming days.

Final Personal Study

Day 1: It's Complicated

Have you ever met up with a friend, and you can tell right away that he or she is distressed, agitated, and frustrated? So you ask a friendly question: "What's wrong?"

After a deep breath and a long sigh, you hear this response: "It's complicated."

What the person is really saying is this: "I don't know where to start. I don't have the energy to explain all the details. It's just — too much."

I think a lot of Christians, a lot of Jesus-followers, live in this place in their relationship to God and his plan for their lives. Their emotional disposition is one of complexity and confusion. They want to live right, but they think, *It's too much. It's too hard.*

Life is complex. There's no doubt about that. It has so many layers, and the older you get, the more complicated and complex it becomes. But often we superimpose the complexity of life on our relationship with God. Before we realize it, we are stressed and tense and wound up about our walk with him.

Have you ever seen a rubber band ball? I had a really odd teacher in junior high whose crowning achievement at the end of the year was that he had made a rubber band ball for the class. I think we all knew he didn't do it for us. He did it for himself.

A lot of people look like that rubber band ball. They have so many layers. They are stretched and tangled and wound up and complex. They don't enjoy God; they don't enjoy their salvation; and they don't enjoy life.

I think preachers can be the worst perpetrators. In an attempt to help people deal with the complexities of life, we create lists, steps, keys, characteristics, points, and principles that are supposed to make us successful. No one can keep up with all that. We end up making Christianity the exclusive right of the devoted, disciplined few. Ultimately this leads to exasperation, and people end up throwing everything out the window because it's too much. It's too complicated.

I'm not questioning those steps and principles. In general they are good, true, and helpful. But I meet too many people who are intimidated — not so much by God, but by a complicated Christianity. They conclude that in order to follow Jesus, they have to study more. They have to know more. They have to practice more.

Jesus came to unravel the myths about God. His life reveals the simplicity of God's love for humanity.

There's an interesting passage in John 14 that illustrates how we tend to complicate the simplicity of the gospel:

> "Don't let your hearts be troubled. Trust in God, and trust also in me. There is more than enough room in my Father's home. If this were not so, would I have told you that I am going to prepare a place for you? When everything is ready, I will come and get you, so that you will always be with me where I am. And you know the way to where I am going."
>
> "No, we don't know, Lord," Thomas said. "We have no idea where you are going, so how can we know the way?"
>
> Jesus told him, "I am the way, the truth, and the life. No one can come to the Father except through me. If you had really known me, you would know who my Father is. From now on, you do know him and have seen him!" (John 14:1–7).

Notice that Jesus is speaking to his disciples about heaven, and he tells them that they know the way to get there. But Thomas objects. Strongly. "No we *don't* know, Lord. We have no idea what you're talking about. We need to know more. We need details. We need dates. We need data. You're stressing us out, Lord."

It's the perfect illustration of human nature. Jesus is standing there in flesh and blood. He is the way to heaven. He is the way to the Father. That's been his message to his disciples for years. But that's too easy. So Thomas complicates it. "Lord, no, we don't know. Explain it. Illustrate it. Diagram it. Please!"

"Thomas," Jesus says, "I am the way. I am the truth. I am the life. I am the way to the Father. I am the way to heaven and eternal life. Everything starts with me and goes through me. It really is that easy."

Life might be complex, but Jesus isn't. His love isn't. His forgiveness isn't.

And when we learn to embrace the simple reality of his grace, we find ourselves enjoying God more than ever.

- Have you ever felt like God or Christianity was too complicated? If so, what was hard to understand?

- Why is it important to keep the gospel uncomplicated?

- How does the simplicity of Jesus help us navigate a complex life?

Day 2: Taste and See

I don't know about you, but I like to know what I'm eating. That's a fair request, isn't it? I enjoy gourmet food and international cuisine, but only if I know exactly what it is that I'm ingesting and digesting.

I don't mean to pick on any one nation, but for some reason French restaurants are among the worst at explaining themselves to foreigners. I'm not talking about restaurants in France, either — that's understandable. I'm talking about restaurants in the United States of America, where the average guy, me included, does not speak a whole lot of French.

The food is probably exquisite. Foodies everywhere are probably rolling their eyes right now. But, like I said, I need to know what I'm eating. If I can't read what's on the menu, pronounce what's on the menu, or understand what's on the menu, can you blame me for not being excited about ordering anything on the menu?

Let's be honest. No menu or description, no matter how eloquent or elaborate, can really describe taste. Even if you know every ingredient and the item is sitting on the plate in front of you, you really don't know what it is like until you try it. You have to taste it for yourself.

Sorry for bringing up small children again, but because a large part of my existence revolves around them these days, I guess it's inevitable. In terms of amazing accomplishments, getting a child to try something new has to rank right up there with the discovery of quantum physics.

"Just try it. You'll like it. I promise."

Let me tell you something. Your kid might be stubborn, but he isn't dumb. He knows you can't promise that he will like it. And the very fact that you promised he would like it *guarantees* he won't like it. Even if he does like it. Welcome to Childrearing Logic 101.

David wrote in Psalm 34:8, "Taste and see that the LORD is good." It's a simple sentence, but I think it's one of the most profound truths ever expressed. God's goodness must be experienced. It must be lived. It must be enjoyed.

We could spend hours, days, months, and years talking about and debating God. We could interview thousands of people and ask what their opinion and experience is of God. We could analyze the logical and psychological and geological and anthropological evidence for God.

But nothing compares to actually experiencing God.

The idea of experiencing God might seem even more abstract than a French menu, but it's actually simple, because God took the initiative to introduce himself to us. He made it easy to experience him. He even dealt with the sin that had separated us from him.

If you want to know what God is like, look at Jesus. For thirty-some years, he lived as God among us. He showed us that we could know him, love him, laugh with him, and learn from him.

When Jesus was about to return to heaven, he told his disciples he was leaving, but that he was not leaving them alone. They didn't understand it at the time, but he was speaking of the Holy Spirit:

"I will ask the Father, and he will give you another Helper, to be with you forever, even the Spirit of truth, whom the world cannot receive, because it neither sees him nor knows him. You know him, for he dwells with you and will be in you. I will not leave you as orphans; I will come to you" (John 14:16–18 ESV).

The Holy Spirit is the invisible but very real presence of God in our lives today. He comforts us, guides us, helps us, and teaches us.

That can seem confusing, I know. It sounds like God is having an identity crisis. Is Jesus God? Or is the Holy Spirit God? Or is the Father God? The answer, of course, is *yes*. They are all God, yet there is only one God. He just happens to consist of three distinct yet completely inseparable "persons," each of whom is totally God.

The fact that God is hard to understand only underscores the fact that he is God and we are human. We will never be able to fully understand him. I can't describe him any better than I can describe foie gras or ravioli or pad thai or enchiladas.

But we can experience him. We can enjoy him. We can revel in him and in his love for us. And I can tell you that once you've tasted God's goodness, nothing else will ever satisfy.

• Have you experienced God in your life? In what way?

- How would you describe God to someone else?

- How would you describe the Holy Spirit's involvement in your day-to-day existence?

Day 3: Follow Me

The other day, my family and another family ran to a local cupcake shop. Literally, we ran. It was a last-minute decision, and the place was going to close in ten minutes. So, four adults and nine children — yes, nine — were running through the streets praying out loud that the shop would stay open.

We made it just in time. There were all these variations of cupcakes. I was like, "Eggnog? Yes! Pumpkin spice? Absolutely!" One cupcake was called Dance Party. I wanted to buy three.

They also had ice cream. Did I get a cone? No, because I'm on a diet. But I might have sampled every flavor twice.

Anyway, the whole carbs thing quickly got out of hand. At one point, one of my friends got an entire cup of the most lethal part of the cupcake: the frosting. *Maple* frosting. That is officially giving up on life. Did we help her eat it? Of course. That's what friends are for. Weep with those who weep and eat with those who eat. So we dove into the maple frosting, and it was a spiritual experience.

Obviously, we made some poor life choices that night. But it was awesome while it lasted. Later, regret and remorse moved in. I was like, "We shouldn't have gone there. We shouldn't have eaten all that. I hate that place. I hate my life. I feel bloated."

I blame God. Why did he have to make it like this? Everything that tastes good makes you feel terrible afterward. And everything that feels terrible — like exercise and diets and self-control in general — makes you feel good afterward.

The same principle seems to be repeated throughout life. We all know we should live a morally sound, socially responsible, generous lifestyle. But it's hard to make the choices that lead to that. It's far easier to make selfish, shortsighted choices that feel good in the moment but that end up coming back to haunt us.

When it comes to enjoying life, we seem to undermine ourselves all the time. We make decisions that short-circuit the goals we are trying to achieve. Instead of long-term satisfaction, we end up settling for short-term enjoyment.

Once you do that enough times, you realize it's an empty way to live. It's unsatisfying and unfulfilling. But how can we live differently? I'm not just talking about laying off the carbs, though that might be a worthy goal. I'm talking about being able to make wise, healthy, holy, morally productive choices. I'm talking about making the people and the world around us better because we are here.

The secret is not self-control. It's not self-discipline. It's not self-improvement. It's not *self* at all. As a matter of fact, self is the problem. The more we focus on self, the worse off we become.

The secret is focusing on Jesus. I know that might sound simplistic, but it really works. As we focus on him, get to know him, and relate to him, we naturally become more like him. We live like he did here on earth. We think like he thinks. We react like he reacts.

Jesus said this: "If anyone would come after me, let him deny himself and take up his cross and follow me" (Mark 8:34 ESV). When we read that, we often focus on the "deny himself and take up his cross" part. We think the answer is to try harder, to force ourselves to change. But this verse starts and ends with the phrases "come after *me*" and "follow *me*."

The emphasis is not on us. It's on Jesus. We accomplish the denying and the taking up through Jesus — through following him, looking at him, and knowing him.

As we follow Jesus, life gets better. It gets more enjoyable. It gets more fulfilling. As we learn to focus on and enjoy Jesus, we learn to enjoy life.

- Is it hard for you to make right choices? What are some areas you've been able to change in? What are some areas you still struggle in?

- How does focusing on Jesus help you be a better version of yourself?

- Practically, what does it mean to "come after" Jesus or "follow" Jesus?

Day 4: Full of Grace and Truth

Have you ever noticed that the hardest people to be gracious to are family members? It's easier to be nice to total strangers than to the people we live with and know the best.

When I meet new people, I just naturally assume the best about them. Even if they are mean and rude, it's not too hard for me to give them the benefit of the doubt. "He's probably just having a bad day." "I bet she has a great heart."

But family? Friends? People I see every day? I love them and I'm loyal to them, but for some reason it's a lot harder to blindly believe the best about them. They say one thing wrong and instantly I'm thinking, *Really? There they go again. So manipulative. So selfish.*

Or maybe a friend of yours comes up to you and says something like this: "Bro, I just met your uncle, and he is amazing. You are so lucky to have an uncle like that." And you're thinking, *He is? I am? Wait, are you sure we're talking about the same guy here?*

He goes on. "Your whole family is just incredible. I can't believe it. I bet you're so thankful for them." And you're like, "Um, yeah, totally thankful." Inside you're thinking, *My family? You have no idea.*

It's so easy to be dumb and gracious. It's so easy when you don't know the nitty-gritty, behind-the-scenes, dirty details. *Oh, he means well. God bless his little soul. He has such a good heart.*

But when it's your kids, your spouse, family members? *No, I'm not giving them the benefit of the doubt. I know what they're doing. They're working the system. They're playing me. I'm not letting them get away with that.*

The more facts I know about people, the more I tend to get frustrated with them. It's hard to believe the best about their bad behavior because I know better. This is exactly what makes Jesus so amazing. The apostle John describes Jesus, whom he refers to poetically as the Word, this way:

> The Word became flesh and dwelt among us, and we have seen his glory, glory as of the only Son from the Father, *full of grace and truth.* (John bore witness about him, and cried out, "This was he of whom I said, 'He who comes after me ranks before me, because he was before me.'") For from his *fullness* we have all received, *grace upon grace.* For the law was given through Moses; *grace and truth* came through Jesus Christ (John 1:14–17 ESV, emphasis added).

Note the emphasized words: *full of grace and truth, fullness, grace upon grace.* Jesus was full of grace and truth.

When I'm full of grace, I'm not so full of truth — that is, details and facts. I'm really good at being full of grace when I'm low on truth. On the other hand, when I'm really truthful, I don't have as much grace. I can be great at telling people the truth, but there isn't a whole lot of grace mixed in, because they don't deserve it. Can you relate?

Sometimes we think Jesus was 50 percent truth and 50 percent grace. We think he was constantly balancing the two, like a good cop/bad cop routine, but all in the same person. He would meet sinners and part of him would want to hug them and part of him would want to punch them.

So we end up doing the same thing. Maybe we've been extra nice lately, so we feel we have to lay down the law just to keep people on their toes. Or we lost our temper over some mistake, so we try to make up for it by being over-the-top sweet for a while.

Not Jesus. He isn't schizophrenic. He isn't bipolar. He doesn't strain to balance grace and truth. He's completely gracious and completely truthful at the same time, all the time. Our human tendency is to limit our grace based on our truth, but God does just the opposite. As Paul wrote in Romans 5:20, "Where sin increased, grace increased all the more."

God knows everything about you and me, but it only makes him love us more. He gives us the benefit of the doubt when he knows we don't deserve it. He believes in us even when we stumble time after time. He loves us eternally, unconditionally, and passionately despite having full knowledge of the darkest corners of our lives. He knows what we've done, what we're doing, and what we're going to do, yet he continuously and fully extends us his grace.

Can you think of anything more extraordinary?

- How would you define grace? How would you define truth?

- Is it hard for you to overlook the mistakes of people who are close to you? Why?

- Is it hard for you to forgive yourself when you make a mistake? How does knowing that God loves you even though he knows everything about you help you live free from condemnation and guilt?

- What does Romans 5:20 mean to you personally?

Day 5: Tell Me What to Do

I am willing to admit publicly that I am a momma's boy. In the most mature, masculine sort of way, of course, but I am. I love my mom. I think she's beautiful, talented, and amazing.

Up until I was about nineteen years old, my mom kept my life fairly uncomplicated. I didn't have to wonder too much about what I was going to do, where I was going to go, or even who I was going to be. I spent the first two decades of my life doing what my mom told me to do. You could chalk it up to being the last-born, the baby of the family. I was a pleaser. I wanted my dad and mom to be happy.

When I was nineteen, my cousin Jon and I worked at a local golf course. We were on the grounds crew and were helping build a new golf course. It was a great job. We found a lot of golf balls while we were working. Is that wrong? Don't judge me.

One day, my mom told me a custodial job had opened up at the City Church, where my parents pastored. I told her I liked my job at the golf course, but I'd also love to work at the church.

Then I said these words: "Mom, just tell me what to do."

You have to understand that for nineteen years, this had been the story of my life. Actually, I didn't even have to say, "Tell me what to do." She would just do it.

She replied, "You know, son, you need to pray about this and make your own decision."

I thought, *What is this, the Twilight Zone? Is she an alien? What did they do with my mother?*

Ultimately, I decided to become a custodian at the church. While we're on the topic, I don't wish on anyone the task of cleaning a women's restroom. Ever. I pray it never happens to you. Am I scarred? Absolutely.

It seems to me that much of humanity approaches God and religion with the mind-set, "Just tell me what to do." John 6 records an encounter between Jesus and a group of people who asked that very question. They had just watched him feed more than five thousand people with a little boy's lunch. They are starting to figure out this guy isn't just a good man and a good teacher — he has a direct connection to God. He might even be the Messiah, the promised savior from God.

I'm sure they are hoping for more free food, but that's not their real goal. I think they realize Jesus can offer them true satisfaction in life. He can help them enjoy life and know God.

That's Jesus' goal as well. Not carbs — but true life. Here is part of their conversation:

> "Do not work for the food that perishes, but for the food that endures to eternal life, which the Son of Man will give to you. For on him God the Father has set his seal."
>
> Then they said to him, "What must we do, to be doing the works of God?"
>
> Jesus answered them, "This is the work of God, that you believe in him whom he has sent" (John 6:27–29 ESV).

For thousands of years, the Jewish people had been used to being told what to do. Their lives revolved around the Ten Commandments and the Law. So here, they approach Jesus expecting something similar. They expect him to tell them what to do to approach God and please God. They want steps. They want principles. They want signs.

But Jesus gives them what must have felt like a frustrating reply: "Believe in him whom he has sent." He's talking about himself, of course. "Here's the work you have to do: trust me." *What?*

Their request is representative of humanity. We want to know exactly what to do to draw close to God. Tell us what to say, what to pray, what to change. Give us action items. Give us something to do.

But God gives us someone to trust.

In other words, true fulfillment in life can never come from checking off a moral to-do list. It can never come from acting a certain way. It can never come from good works or long prayers or empty rituals.

True fulfillment comes from relationship with God through Jesus. Later in this conversation, Jesus calls himself the Bread of Life. His point is that just as we get natural life from bread — or donuts, for some of us — so we receive spiritual life through him.

The source of eternal life is Jesus, not works. Christianity is not about a to-do list. It's not about performance. It's about Jesus. It's about trusting in him, following him, and knowing him.

When we know him, our lives will change. We will find ourselves thinking, talking, and acting differently than before. It's impossible to truly know Jesus and not start walking in the new life and new lifestyle he offers us. And we'll like the "new us" a lot better, I might add.

But our behavior isn't the essence of Christianity. It's not the starting place or the goal of our walk with God. The essence of Christianity is Jesus. Just as he did with this group of people two thousand years ago, he invites you to have faith in him.

That is the beginning of true life.

- Why do you think people tend to emphasize *doing* when it comes to God and religion? How is Jesus' message in John 6:29 about the "work of God" different?

- Even if we could live a perfectly moral life on our own, do you think that would be satisfying without knowing Jesus personally? Why or why not?

- What does the phrase "the essence of Christianity is Jesus" mean to you? How does that truth affect your day-to-day lifestyle?

"Judah is the most compassionate and giving person I have ever met. His teachings are easy to understand and full of truth and real life."

—Bubba Watson,
Two-time Masters Champion

jesusisbook.com

lifeisbook.tv